ELEMENTARY KOREAN II
ACTIVITY BOOK

First Edition

Jiyoung Kim, Ph.D.
Indiana University Bloomington

cognella®
SAN DIEGO

Bassim Hamadeh, CEO and Publisher
Angela Schultz, Senior Field Acquisitions Editor
Albert Liau, Project Editor
Jordan Krikorian, Editorial Associate
Alia Bales, Associate Production Manager
Jess Estrella, Graphic Design
Alexa Lucido, Licensing Manager
Natalie Piccotti, Director of Marketing
Kassie Graves, Senior Vice President, Editorial
Jamie Giganti, Director of Academic Publishing

Cover image copyright © 2014 Depositphotos/yienkeat.

Printed in the United States of America.

cognella® | ACADEMIC PUBLISHING
3970 Sorrento Valley Blvd., Ste. 500, San Diego, CA 92121

CONTENTS

CHAPTER 1. MEETING CLASSMATES AFTER WINTER BREAK

겨울 방학 재미있었지요?

OBJECTIVES

- You will be able to exchange a dialogue about a break on the 1st day of the new semester.
- You will be able to confirm what you think classmates did during the break.
- You will be able to talk about classes to take in the new semester.
- You will be able to talk about housing plans for a new semester.

KEY EXPRESSIONS AND STRUCTURES

- V ~지요?: Sentence ending for confirmation
- 겨울 방학 재미있었지요?: Did you have a nice vacation, didn't you?
- 이번 학기에 몇 과목 들어요?: How many courses are you taking this semester?
- 수업이 언제 있어요?: When do you have class?
- 이번 학기에도 기숙사에 살아요?: Do you live in a dormitory this semester as well?

TASK: MEETING CLASSMATES AFTER WINTER BREAK

On the 1st day the spring semester, you meet classmates and talk about what you did during the break and your plans for a new semester.

PRACTICE QUESTIONS

1. 겨울 방학 어땠어요? **집에 갔지요?**
2. 크리스마스에 뭐 했어요? **재미있었지요?**
3. 크리스마스 선물도 많이 **받았지요?**
4. 이번 학기에 **몇 과목 들어요? 무슨 수업 들어요?**
5. 이번 학기에 **수업이 언제 있어요?**
6. **이번 학기에도 기숙사에 살아요?**

ACTIVITY 1: 새 학기에 다시 만난 친구들과 이야기해 보세요.

On the 1st day the spring semester, meet your classmates and talk about what you did during the winter break.

[모델 대화]

마이클:　　에밀리 씨, 겨울 방학 잘 보냈어요? 반가워요!

에밀리:　　네, 반가워요! 마이클 씨도 겨울 방학 잘 보냈어요?

마이클:　　네, 잘 보냈어요. 에밀리 씨는 겨울 방학에 뭐 했어요?

에밀리:　　저는 집에서 가족하고 같이 시간을 보냈어요.

　　　　　　마이클 씨도 겨울 방학에 집에 갔지요?

마이클:　　네, 저도 집에 갔어요. 가족하고 같이 크리스마스 파티를 했어요.

　　　　　　에밀리 씨도 크리스마스 재미있었지요?

에밀리:　　네, 크리스마스 파티도 하고 선물도 받았어요.

_____

_____

_____

_____

_____

_____

ACTIVITY 2: 새 학기에 듣는 수업에 대해 이야기 해 보세요.

Talk about classes you are taking in the new semester. Ask your classmates how many courses and what kind of courses they are taking, what time their classes are, who their new professors are, and so forth.

[모델 대화]

마이클:　　　에밀리 씨, 이번 학기에도 수업 많이 듣**지요?**

에밀리:　　　네, 많이 들어요.

마이클:　　　**몇 과목 들어요?**

에밀리:　　　세 과목 들어요.

마이클:　　　**무슨 수업 들어요?**

에밀리:　　　한국어 수업하고 한국 역사 수업하고 심리학 수업을 들어요.

마이클:　　　한국 역사 수업 선생님이 누구세요?

에밀리:　　　제임스 박 선생님이세요.

마이클:　　　**수업이 언제 있어요?**

에밀리:　　　화요일하고 목요일 오후 4 시 10 분에 있어요.

_____

_____

_____

_____

_____

_____

_____

ACTIVITY 3: 새 학기에 사는 집과 룸메이트에 대해 이야기 해 보세요.

Talk about housing plans for a new semester. Ask your classmates if there is any change in their housing in the new semester as well as possible roommates.

[모델 대화]

마이클: 에밀리 씨, **이번 학기에도 기숙사에 살아요?**

에밀리: 아니요, 이번 학기에는 기숙사에 안 살고 아파트에 살아요.

마이클: 아, 그래요? 아파트는 괜찮아요?

에밀리: 네, 아주 넓고 깨끗해요.

마이클: 방이 몇 개 있어요?

에밀리: 두 개 있어요.

마이클: 아, 그래요? 그럼, 룸메이트도 있어요?

에밀리: 네, 한 명 있어요.

           제 룸메이트도 인디애나 대학교 학생이에요.

_____

_____

_____

_____

_____

_____

_____

WRAP-UP ACTIVITY

Write about what you did during the winter break and your plans for the new semester. Include classes you are taking in the new semester as well as your housing arrangements. Then, present your writing to the class.

[모델 작문]

저는 겨울 방학에 집에 갔어요. 가족하고 같이 크리스마스 파티를 했어요. 크리스마스 선물을 많이 받았어요. 고등학교 친구들도 만났어요. 친구들하고 같이 이야기도 하고 영화도 봤어요. 겨울 방학이 참 재미있었어요.

이번 봄 학기에도 수업을 많이 들어요. 다섯 과목을 들어요. 한국어 수업, 한국 역사 수업, 한국 문화 수업, 수학 수업, 그리고 피아노 수업을 들어요. 이번 학기도 아주 바쁠 거예요.

이번 학기에는 기숙사에 안 살고 아파트에 살아요. 아파트는 학교에서 아주 가까워요. 걸어서 15 분 걸려요. 아파트가 아주 넓고 깨끗해요. 방은 두 개 있고 룸메이트가 한 명 있어요. 룸메이트도 인디애나 대학교 학생이에요.

_____

_____

_____

_____

_____

_____

CULTURAL AWARENESS: BEGINNING OF THE SEMESTER AT A KOREAN SCHOOL
한국 대학의 학기 시작

Schools in Korea begin their first semester in March. Many schools hold a matriculation ceremony for new students around then. At the ceremony, parents, relatives, and friends as well as the new students come to celebrate entering the new school. So, on the day of the ceremony, you can see many shops selling flowers around the school. After the ceremony, students might eat jajangmyeon (짜장면) with parents and friends who came to celebrate. This is because 짜장면 is traditionally a food that Koreans ate on special occasions. But these days, there are many more delicious and special foods, so there are other options besides 짜장면.

As for university, many freshmen attend welcoming parties and semester opening parties at the beginning of the semester, as well. These parties are often held by departments and clubs and are held in large classrooms or auditoriums after class, or even in rented out restaurants or coffee shops. And since there are big and small school opening parties all over the school at the beginning of the semester, March often passes by quickly.

Figure 1.1 Matriculation Ceremony

Credit
Fig. 1.1: Copyright © by 세종사이버대학교 (CC BY-ND 2.0) at https://flic.kr/p/24pZuHV.

CHAPTER 2. GIVING AND RECEIVING PRESENTS
크리스마스 선물 많이 받았어요?

OBJECTIVES

- You will be able to talk about what kind of gift you received on Christmas and from whom.
- You will be able to talk about what kind of gift you gave on Christmas and to whom.
- You will be able to interview your classmates about gifts they receive and give and email messages they send and receive.
- You will be able to write about what you did on Christmans.

KEY EXPRESSIONS AND STRUCTURES

- 크리스마스에 선물 받았어요?: Did you get a Christmas gift?
- 무슨 선물 받았어요?: What kind of gift did you get?
- 누구한테서 선물 받았어요?: Whom did you get a gift from?
- 누구한테 선물했어요/줬어요?: Whom did you give a gift to?
- 어머니날: Mother's Day, 아버지날: Father's Day, 어버이날: Parents' Day
- 지난: last, 작년: last year, 올해: this year, 내년: next year

TASK: TAKING ABOUT GIVING AND RECEIVING GIFTS

Talk about giving and receiving gifts on Christmas and on your birthday, including what kind of gift you received and from whom, and what kind of gift you gave and to whom.

PRACTICE QUESTIONS

1. 크리스마스 선물 많이 받았어요?
2. 무슨 선물 받았어요?
3. 누구한테서 선물 받았어요?
4. 크리스마스에 **누구한테 선물 줬어요?**
5. 무슨 선물 줬어요?

ACTIVITY 1: 크리스마스에 받은 선물에 대해 이야기해 보세요.

Talk about giving and receiving Christmas gifts. Ask each other what kind of gift you received on Christmas Day and from whom.

[모델 대화]

미나: 유미 씨, 크리스마스 재미있었어요? 뭐 했어요?

유미: 가족하고 같이 크리스마스 파티 했어요.

미나: **크리스마스 선물도 많이 받았어요?**

유미: 네, 많이 받았어요.

미나: **무슨 선물을 받았어요?**

유미: 책하고 돈을 받았어요.

미나: **누구한테서 받았어요?**

유미: 동생한테서 책을 받고 어머니께 돈을 받았어요.

_____

_____

_____

_____

_____

_____

_____

ACTIVITY 2: 지난 생일에 받은 선물에 대해서 이야기해 보세요.

Talk about birthday gifts. First ask your partner when their birthday is and what they did on their birthday. Then ask what kind of gift they received and from whom.

[모델 대화]

미나: 유미 씨, 생일이 언제예요?

유미: 9월 15일이에요.

미나: 작년 생일에 뭐 했어요?

유미: 친구들하고 생일 파티 했어요.

미나: **생일 선물도 많이 받았어요?**

유미: 네, 많이 받았어요.

미나: **무슨 선물을 받았어요?**

유미: 제니한테서 가방을 선물 받았어요.

_____

_____

_____

_____

_____

_____

_____

_____

ACTIVITY 3: 주고 받은 선물과 이메일에 대해 이야기 해 보세요.

Interview classmates about gifts they receive and give, and email messages they receive and send. Report on the interviews after they are completed.

INTERVIEW QUESTIONS

1. 크리스마스 선물:	1) 지난 크리스마스에 누구한테서 선물 받았어요?
	2) 지난 크리스마스에 누구한테 선물 줬어요?
2. 생일 선물:	1) 지난 생일에 누구한테서 선물 받았어요?
	2) 누구한테 생일 선물 줬어요?
3. 이메일:	1) 누구한테서 자주 이메일을 받아요?
	2) 누구한테 자주 이메일을 써요?
4. 문자 메시지:	1) 누구한테서 자주 문자 메세지를 받아요?
	2) 누구한테 자주 문자 메시지를 보내요?

SAMPLE INTERVIEW ANSWERS

친구 이름:	에밀리
1. 크리스마스 선물:	1) 지난 크리스마스에 동생한테서 책을 선물 받았어요.
	2) 지난 크리스마스에 친구한테 가방을 선물했어요.
2. 생일 선물:	1) 지난 생일에 유미한테서 옷을 받았어요
	2) 어머니 생신에 어머니께 꽃을 드렸어요.
3. 이메일:	1) 선생님께 자주 이메일을 받아요.
	2) 언니한테 자주 이메일을 써요.
4. 문자 메시지:	1) 제니한테 자주 문자 메시지를 받아요.
	2) 동생한테 자주 문자 메시지를 보내요.

INTERVIEW SHEET

친구 이름:	
1. 크리스마스 선물:	1) 지난 크리스마스에 누구한테서 선물 받았어요? 2) 지난 크리스마스에 누구한테 선물 줬어요?
2. 생일 선물:	1) 지난 생일에 누구한테서 선물 받았어요? 2) 누구한테 생일 선물 줬어요?
3. 이메일:	1) 누구한테서 자주 이메일을 받아요? 2) 누구한테 자주 이메일을 써요?
4. 문자 메시지:	1) 누구한테서 자주 문자 메세지를 받아요? 2) 누구한테 자주 문자 메시지를 보내요?

REPORT

1. 에밀리 씨는 지난 크리스마스에 동생한테서 책을 선물 받았어요. 그리고 친구한테 가방을 선물 했어요.

2. 에밀리 씨는 지난 생일에 유미한테서 옷을 선물 받았어요. 그리고 어머니 생신에 어머니께 꽃을 드렸어요.

3. 에밀리 씨는 선생님께 자주 이메일을 받아요. 그리고 언니한테 자주 이메일을 써요.

4. 에밀리 씨는 제니한테 자주 문자 메시지를 받아요. 그리고 동생한테 자주 문자 메시지를 보내요

_____

_____

_____

_____

_____

_____

_____

_____

WRAP-UP ACTIVITY

Write about what you did on Christmans. Include what kind of gifts you received and from whom and what kind of gifts you gave and to whom. Then, present your writing to the class.

[모델 작문]

지난 크리스마스에 가족들하고 크리스마스 파티를 했어요. 크리스마스 선물을 많이 받았어요. 동생한테서 책을 받고 어머니께 돈을 받았어요. 그리고 저는 동생한테 예쁜 공책을 선물하고 어머니께 따뜻한 스카프를 선물했어요. 맛있는 크리스마스 케이크하고 치킨도 먹었어요. 그리고 동생하고 같이 '나 홀로 집에'[1] 영화를 봤어요. 아주 재미있는 영화였어요.

_____

_____

_____

_____

_____

_____

_____

_____

_____

[1] 나 홀로 집에: Korean title of the movie *Home Alone*

CULTURAL AWARENESS: CHRISTMAS IN KOREA 한국의 크리스마스

Christmas was first introduced in Korea by Protestant missionaries in the late 1800s and began to spread in earnest through Western-style schools and churches. Since then, Christmas has been recognized as one of the most important anniversaries in Korea just like Western countries. Starting in early December, people decorate streets and shops with Christmas lights and trees, and Christmas carols play everywhere on TV and radio. The difference between Christmas in Korea and the West is that Christmas in Korea is a day for a young people to gather together rather than families gathering. On Christmas day, people go out to see their friends and enjoy the Christmas spirits, having Christmas parties and watching Christmas events and music concerts. Most shops and businesses are closed on Christmas Day in America, but in Korea all the shops and markets are crowded because it's the Christmas rush. No heavy traffic jams are expected on Christmas Day, unlike traditional holidays when all the roads are overflowing with cars going to their hometown. Instead, a lot of cars are seen on the roads to go to vacation spots such as ski resorts and golf courses. If you spend Christmas in Korea, you will experience a fancy and bustling holiday.

Figure 2.1. Street view on Christmas in Korea

Credit

CHAPTER 3. MAKING PLANS FOR SPRING BREAK
봄 방학에 뭐 하고 싶어요?

OBJECTIVES

- You will be able to talk about what you want to do for spring break.
- You will be able to make plans for leisure activities.
- You will be able to make plans with your friends and family.
- You will be able to suggest leisure activities to friends.

KEY EXPRESSIONS AND STRUCTURES

- V ~고 싶다: I'd like to V/I want to V/I wish to V
- 뭐 하고 싶어요?: What would you like to do?
- 주말에 뭐 할 거예요?: What are you going to do this weekend?
- 같이 가요!: Let's go together!

TASK: TALKING ABOUT THINGS YOU'D LIKE TO DO FOR YOUR LEISURE TIME

Talk about what you'd like to do for your free time/weekend/vacation and make plans with your friends. Suggest activities such as going to a park, going see a movie, going to a restaurant, and so on.

PRACTICE QUESTIONS

Ask the following questions and find out what your partner wants to do:

1. 오늘 저녁에 뭐 먹고 **싶어요?**
2. 이번 주말에 뭐 하고 **싶어요?**
3. 봄 방학에 어디 가고 **싶어요?**
4. 생일에 무슨 선물을 받고 **싶어요?**
5. 주말에 무슨 영화 보고 **싶어요?**

ACTIVITY 1: 다가오는 봄방학에 하고 싶은 것을 이야기해 보세요.

First talk about what you want to do for spring break, as the break is just around the corner. Then talk about what you want in the following situations:

- What you want to do during summer
- What you want to do after graduation[2]

[모델 대화]

유진:	미나 씨, 봄 방학에 **뭐 하고 싶어요?**
미나:	글쎄요, 아직 잘 모르겠어요. 유진 씨는요?
유진:	저는 하와이에 여행 가고 **싶어요?**
미나:	아, 그래요? 하와이에서 뭐 하고 **싶어요?**
유진:	수영도 하고 서핑도 하고 **싶어요.**
미나:	와! 저도 하와이에 가고 **싶어요.**

_____

_____

_____

_____

_____

_____

_____

[2] Graduation: 졸업, to graduate: 졸업하다, after graduation: 졸업하고

ACTIVITY 2: 이번 주말 계획에 대해서 이야기 해 보세요.

Suppose that you have plans for this coming weekend as in the following situations. Dialogue with your partner about the following situation:

- Your parents come and visit you this weekend.
- You want to go see a movie with a friend.
- Your friend's birthday is this Saturday. You are having a birthday party for him.

[모델 대화]

유진:	미나 씨, **이번 주말에 뭐 할 거예요?**
미나:	저는 다음 주에 시험이 있어서 도서관에서 공부할 거예요.
유진:	아, 시험이 있어요?
미나:	네, 한국어 수업을 듣는데 시험이 많아요. 유진 씨는요?
유진:	저는 이번 주말에 시카고에서 언니가 와요.
	언니하고 같이 이야기도 하고 시간을 많이 보내**고 싶어요.**
미나:	네, 그럼 주말 잘 보내세요!

_____

_____

_____

_____

_____

_____

_____

_____

ACTIVITY 3: 시험 끝나고 하고 싶은 일을 제안해 보세요.

Talk about what you want to do after a Korean test tomorrow. Suggest to your parter doing something together, such as the following:

- Going to a park together. You want to ride a bicycle at the park.
- Going to a mall together. You want to get a birthday gift for your mom.
- Going to a Korean restaurant together. You want to have spicy[3] food at the restaurant.

[모델 대화]

유진: 미나 씨, 내일 한국어 **시험 끝나고 뭐 할 거예요**?

미나: 글쎄요. 재미있는 일 있어요?.

유진: 요즘 날씨가 참 좋은데 저하고 **같이** 공원에 **가요**.

            공원에서 자전거 타**고 싶어요**

미나: 네, 좋아요. 저도 자전거 타**고 싶어요**. 어느 공원에 가요?

유진: 학교 앞 블루밍턴 공원 어때요?

미나: 네, 좋아요. 몇 시에 만나요?

유진: 토요일 오전 10 시에 만나요.

_____

_____

_____

_____

_____

_____

---

[3] To be spicy: 맵다, spicy food: 매운 음식

WRAP-UP ACTIVITY

Write about your plans for spring break/summer vacation. Write all the things that you'd like to do, including places that you wish to travel and people you want to meet during the vacation. After writing, present your plans to the class.

[모델 작문]

저는 이번 여름 방학에 여러 나라를 여행 하고 싶습니다. 한국에 친구들이 많아서 한국에 가고 싶습니다. 한국에서 맛있는 음식도 먹고 친구들도 만나고 싶습니다. 친구들하고 같이 덕수궁과 경복궁[4]도 구경하고[5] 싶습니다. 예쁜 사진도 많이 찍을 거예요. 그리고 전주[6]에 가서 비빔밥을 먹고 싶습니다. 전주 비빔밥은 아주 유명합니다[7].

_____

_____

_____

_____

_____

_____

_____

_____

---

[4] 덕수궁 & 경복궁: Royal palaces in Seoul

[5] 구경하다: to look around

[6] 전주: one of cities in Korea

[7] 유명하다: to be famous

CULTURAL AWARENESS: WHAT KOREAN STUDENTS DO DURING SCHOOL VACATION? 한국 학생들의 방학

The school system in Korea is different than America's. So is school vacation. In Korea, winter vacation (December to February) is a lot longer than summer vacation (July to August). People usually think that students take a break from studying and have fun during the vacation. Korean students, however, spend much of their vacation time studying. They don't just go to school but go to 학원 to study. The main reason they go to 학원 is to prepare for getting a job. In Korea, it is very competitive to get a job, and most companies require them to pass an employment exam. It is very difficult to pass a civil service examination to get a government job. Thus, it is not uncommon to see students study very harder during the school vacation.

As for high school students, they have even busier schedule during the vacation than during the regular semester. Many high schools in Korea offer supplementary lessons (보충 수업), which are mandatory. Also, a lot of 학원 s hold special sessions/lectures during the vacation. Thus, students become busier going to school and 학원 at the same time. As you may know, 학원 s in Seoul provide high-quality lessons to prepare for the SAT. Some Korean students who study abroad come back to Korea during summer to attend 학원 in Seoul.

Of course, there are some students who enjoy their vacation in Korea and take a trip. Some of them go on a backpacking trip. Their most favored sites are within Korea (including Jeju Island), Japan, and Southeast Asian countries. Some go to an English-speaking country to study English. Lots of students study English in the summer to take tests such as the TOEIC, OPIC, and TOEFL. They may take part in summer student-exchange programs.

Figure 3.1 Vacation 방학

Credit

CHAPTER 4. GIVING REASONS WHY
왜 한국어를 배워요?

OBJECTIVES

- You will be able to dialogue about why you are learning Korean.
- You will be able to say good things and bad things about your home.
- You will be able to make an excuse for various situations such as not coming to a party, being later for class, not doing homework, and so on.
- You will be able to write and give a presentation on good things and bad things about your city.

KEY EXPRESSIONS AND STRUCTURES

- V/A ~어서/아서 (Clausal connective): because/since
- V/A ~고 싶어서: because/since I want to V/A
- V/A ~어서/아서 좋아요/안 좋아요: It is good/not good because V/A
- V/A ~어서/아서 좋아해요/안 좋아해요: I like/don't like it because V/A
- V/A ~어서/아서 편해요/불편해요: It is convenient/inconvenient because V/A

TASK: GIVING REASONS WHY YOU LIKE/DISLIKE SOMETHING

Say your favorite language, season, food, music, movie/TV star, and so on, along with reasons they are your favorites.

PRACTICE QUESTIONS

Ask each other the following questions and give a reason by using ~어서/아서:

1. 한국 음악 좋아해요? 왜 (안) 좋아해요?
2. 주말에 왜 유진 씨 생일 파티에 안 왔어요?
3. 오늘 왜 한국어 수업에 늦었어요?
4. 무슨 전공하고 싶**어서** 인디애나 대학교에 왔어요?
5. 인디애나 대학교 어때요? 좋아요? 왜 (안) 좋아요?

PATTERN PRACTICE 1: REASONS YOU LIKE . . .

Talk about reasons why you like the following things: movie/drama/song/book/sports, TV star/movie star/singer.

- What kind of movie/drama/song/book/sports do your like? Why?
- Who's your favorite TV star/movie star/singer? Why?

[모델 패턴]

A: OO 씨, 좋아하는 가수가 누구예요?

B: BTS 지민이에요.

A: 왜 지민을 좋아해요?

B: 춤을 아주 잘 **춰서** 좋아해요.

_____

_____

_____

PATTERN PRACTICE 2: REASONS YOU CHOSE YOUR SCHOOL

Ask each other about reasons you chose your school.

[모델 패턴]

A: OO 씨, 왜 인디애나 대학교에 왔어요?

B: 저는 한국어를 전공하**고 싶어서** 인디애나 대학교에 왔어요.

_____

_____

_____

ACTIVITY 1: 한국어 수업을 듣는 이유에 대해서 이야기 해 보세요.

Dialogue about why you are learning Korean.

[모델 대화]

데이빗: 에밀리 씨는 왜 한국어를 배우세요?

에밀리: 한국 문화를 **좋아해서** 한국어를 배워요. 데이빗 씨는요?

데이빗: 저는 한국어 수업이 **재미있어서** 배워요.

에밀리: 저도 한국어 수업이 재미있어요.

데이빗: 저는 나중에[8] 한국어를 전공하**고 싶어요**.

에밀리: 그럼, 한국어 공부 열심히 하세요!

_____

_____

_____

_____

_____

_____

_____

---

[8] 나중에: later, in the near future

ACTIVITY 2: 기숙사 생활의 좋은 점과 나쁜 점에 대해서 말해 보세요.

Talk about good and bad things about your living in a dorm or your current home along with the reasons why it is good or bad.

	Positive	Nagative
Your living place: (e.g., 기숙사, 아파트)	학교에서 가깝다	방이 작다
	학교 식당 음식이 맛있다	학교 식당 음식이 비싸다
	룸메이트가 재미있다	룸메이트가 시끄럽다
	아파트 방이 크다	아파트 렌트가 비싸다

[모델 대화]

에밀리: 데이빗 씨, 지금 어디 살아요?

데이빗: 학교 기숙사에 살아요.

에밀리: 그래요? 기숙사 생활이 어때요?

데이빗: 학교에서 **가까워서 좋은데** 방이 작**아서 불편해요.**

에밀리: 아, 그래요? 룸메이트는 어때요?

데이빗: 룸메이트가 재미있**어서** 좋은데 시끄러**워서** 안 좋아요.

_____

_____

_____

_____

_____

_____

_____

ACTIVITY 3: 다음 상황에 대한 변명을 해 보세요.

Suppose that you are in the following situations and make an excuse for each:

- You didn't make it for a birthday party because you had a prior engagement.[9]
- You were late for Korean class because there were heavy traffic jams.[10]
- You didn't go to school yesterday because you had a stomachache.[11]
- You couldn't do your homework for Korean class because you didn't have time.

[모델 대화]

에밀리: 데이빗 씨, 어제 스티브 생일이었는데 파티에 갔어요?

데이빗: 아니요. 어제 오후에 수업이 **있어서** 못 갔어요.

에밀리: 아, 그래요? 저도 못 갔어요.

데이빗: 에밀리 씨는 왜 못 갔어요?

에밀리: 머리가 많이 **아파서** 못 갔어요.

데이빗: 지금은 괜찮아요?

에밀리: 네, 괜찮아요.

_____

_____

_____

_____

_____

---

[9] Prior engagement: 약속

[10] Traffic jams: 교통이 막히다

[11] Stomachache: 배가 아프다

WRAP-UP ACTIVITY

Write about the city you grew up in. Write all the things you like and dislike about the city, including reasons why. Take notes of them in the table that follows and then write your notes in essay form on the next page. After writing, present your essay to the class.

Name of city	Positive	Negative
City you grew up: 블루밍턴	<ul><li>깨끗하다</li><li>차가 많이 없다</li><li>공기가 깨끗하다</li><li>공원이 많다</li><li>음악 콘서트/공연을 자주 볼 수 있다</li><li>대학교가 있다</li><li>Think of your own</li></ul>	<ul><li>공항에서 멀다</li><li>쇼핑몰이 없다</li><li>렌트가 비싸다</li><li>겨울에 춥다</li><li>한국 식당/마켓이 많이 없다</li><li>Think of your own</li></ul>
City you grew up: _____		

[모델 작문]

저는 블루밍턴에서 왔습니다. 블루밍턴은 아주 깨끗한 도시입니다. 차가 많이 **없어서** 공기[12]가 깨끗합니다. 공원이 많고 음악 콘서트가 자주 **있어서** 좋아합니다. 그리고 대학교 캠퍼스가 **있어서** 편리합니다. 그런데, 공항이 **멀어서** 아주 불편합니다. 또, 겨울에 날씨가 너무 **추워서** 안 좋습니다. 한국 식당과 한국 마켓도 많이 **없어서** 불편합니다. 하지만 블루밍턴은 제 **고향이어서** 좋아합니다.

_____

_____

_____

_____

_____

_____

_____

_____

[12] 공기: air

CULTURAL AWARENESS: WHY ARE YOU LEARNING THE KOREAN LANGUAGE?
한국어를 배우는 이유

The number of people learning Korean was highest in 2019. More and more schools in the United States offer Korean language courses along with Korean culture and literature courses. What are their motivations to learn Korean? When I ask people this question most of the time I hear it is because of K-pop or Korean dramas, so-called Hallyu 한류. They wish to understand lyrics of their favorite K-pops and their favorite dramas in Korean.

Another reason is that the Korean economy has been rapidly boosted and has become a global economic power, so more people wish to live and work in Korea. Actually, the number of foreigners living in Korea is considerably increasing, and they have brought a lot of changes in society. New policies and services for foreigners have been adopted to prepare for a multicultural society.

Figure 4.1 K-pop concert.

Credit

CHAPTER 5. MAKING WEEKEND PLANS
주말에 뭐 할까요?

OBJECTIVES

- You will be able to make plans for a weekend and give your opinion by making a suggestion.
- You will be able to offer someone alternatives when asking someone's opinion.
- You will be able to decline someone's offer and suggest another time.
- You will be able to write about and present plans for an upcoming break or vacation.

KEY EXPRESSIONS AND STRUCTURES

- V ~(으)ㄹ까요? (Sentence ender): Shall we V?
- V ~(으)ㄹ래요? (Sentence ender): Would you like to V?
- V1 ~(으)ㄹ까요, V2 ~(으)ㄹ까요?: Shall we V1 or V2?
- 주말에 뭐 할까요?: What shall we do this weekend?

TASK: EXCHANGE OPINIONS ABOUT WEEKEND PLANS BY MAKING SUGGESTIONS

Talk about what you'd like to do with your free time/weekend/vacation and make plans with your friends. Suggest activities such as going to a park, seeing a movie, going to a restaurant, and so on.

PRACTICE QUESTIONS

1. 점심에 뭐 **먹을까요?**
2. 시험 끝나고 오후에 쇼핑하러 **갈래요?**
3. 날씨가 좋은데 바닷가에서 수영**할래요?**
4. 한국어 잘 하고 싶은데 **어떻게 할까요?**
5. 주말에 어디서 공부할까요? 도서관에서 **할까요**, 커피숍에서 **할까요?**

PATTERN PRACTICE 1: SUGGESTING WEEKEND ACTIVITIES BY USING ~(으)ㄹ래요?

- Seeing a movie
- Studying at a library
- Drinking coffee at a cafe
- Going to a park
- Going swimming

[모델 패턴]

A: OO 씨, 이번 주말에 뭐 할까요?

B: 날씨가 좋은데 영화 보러 **갈래요?**

A: 네, 좋아요.

PATTERN PRACTICE 2: ASKING OPINIONS ABOUT WEEKEND PLANS BY USING ~(으)ㄹ까요?

- Seeing a movie or a music concert
- Studying at a library or a coffee shop
- Drinking coffee or tea at a cafe
- Going to a park or beach
- Going hiking or swimming

[모델 패턴]

A: OO 씨, 이번 주말에 영화 **볼까요,** 콘서트에 **갈까요?**

B: '스파이더 맨' 보고 싶은데 영화 보러 가요.

A: 네, 좋아요.

_____

_____

_____

ACTIVITY 1: 휴일 계획을 세우면서 자신의 의견을 제안해 보세요.

Dialogue with your partner about plans for the upcoming holiday, including setting up a time and place to meet. Ask your partner's opinions by making the following suggestions:

- Going to a park
- Seeing a movie
- Inviting friends over and having dinner at your place
- Going to Chicago to eat/buy Korean food at a Korean market

[모델 대화]

마크: 미나 씨, 내일 휴일인데 **뭐 할까요?**

미나: 글쎄요. 마크 씨는 뭐 하고 싶어요?

마크: 저는 공원에 가고 싶은데요.

미나: 그래요? 그럼 공원에 가요!

마크: 공원에서 자전거 **탈까요?**

미나: 네, 좋아요. 그럼, 내일 오후에 공원 앞에서 **만날래요?**

마크: 네, 그래요.

_____

_____

_____

_____

_____

_____

_____

ACTIVITY 2: 선택 사항을 주고 친구의 의견을 물어 보세요.

Exchange opinions about where to study over the weekend. Offer your partner a choice of alternatives by using ~(으)ㄹ까요, ~(으)ㄹ까요?. Also, talk to your partner about the following items:

- Place to study tonight (도서관 or 커피숍)
- Lunch menu to eat today (한국 음식 or 중국 음식)
- Activities for this weekend (영화 or 연극)
- Music to listen to (BTS or Exo)

[모델 대화]

미나:	마크 씨, 한국어 시험이 언제 있어요?
마크:	다음 주 월요일에 있어요.
미나:	그럼, 주말에 **같이 공부 할까요?**
마크:	네, 좋아요. **도서관에서 할까요, 커피숍에서 할까요?**
미나:	커피숍이 **어때요?**
	학교 앞 커피숍이 아주 넓고 좋아요
마크:	네, 그럼 커피숍에서 해요!

_____

_____

_____

_____

_____

_____

_____

ACTIVITY 3: 친구의 주말 계획 제안에 다른 시간을 제안해 보세요.

Suppose that you are in the following situations. Suggest an activity to your partner. Your partner will not make it that day, so offer an alternative time.

- You'd like to see a movie this weekend.
- You'd like to go to a mall to buy new shoes.
- You'd like to eat Bibimbop and thus go to a Korean restaurant.
- You'd like to go to a karaoke bar to sing Korean songs.
- You feel like going to a beach since the weather is nice.

[모델 대화]

마크: 미나 씨, 이번 주말에 시간 있어요?

미나: 주말에요? 왜요?

마크: AMC 극장에서 '스파이더맨'을 하는데 **보러 갈래요?**

미나: 죄송한데 숙제가 많아서 바쁜데요.

마크: 그럼, 다음 주말에 **볼까요?**

미나: 네, 다음 주말은 괜찮아요.

마크: 그럼, 다음주 토요일에 봐요.

미나: 네, 좋아요!

_____

_____

_____

_____

_____

_____

WRAP-UP ACTIVITY

Write about your weekend activities. Include your plans for the coming weekend. Then present your writing to the class.

저는 주말에 보통 아침에 늦게 일어납니다. 아침을 먹고 룸메이트하고 집 청소를 합니다. 오후에는 장 보러 마트에 갑니다. 그리고 룸메이트하고 같이 저녁을 만듭니다. 보통 저녁을 먹고 룸메이트하고 같이 재미있는 영화를 봅니다.

이번 주말에는 언니가 시카고에서 올 거예요. 언니하고 같이 한국 음식을 먹으러 한국 식당에 갈 거예요.

_____

_____

_____

_____

_____

_____

_____

_____

CULTURAL AWARENESS: WHAT DO KOREANS DO FOR LEISURE ACTIVITIES 노래방

What do Koreans usually do for leisure activities? Koreans love to sing and are good at it. When they get together with friends and colleagues, there is one place where they must go: 노래방, a combination of the words 노래 (song) and 방 (room). In other words, 노래방 is the Korean version of karaoke. There is slight difference between traditional karaoke and the Korean one. 노래방 is done in private singing rooms, so perhaps you'd feel more comfortable in these environments because you don't sing on a big stage in front of a bunch of strangers. 노래방 is hugely popular in Korea for all ages, from children to the old. You don't need to go to downtown to go to 노래방; it can be easily found anywhere in town. When you see many signs of 노래방 in Korea, you can imagine how much Koreans love and enjoy singing. It was even written in a history book that Koreans have a lot of 흥 (joy/excitement) and 끼 (talents). It is not difficult to find people who are very good at singing in Korea. That is the reason many K-pop stars/groups have been recognized and gained celebrity status from all over the world. If you have a Korean friend, ask the friend to take you to 노래방. I am sure you will have fun!

Figure 5.1 노래방

Credit

Fig. 5.1: Copyright © 2016 Pixabay/955169.

CHAPTER 6. TALKING ABOUT COLLEGE LIFE
대학 생활이 어때요?

OBJECTIVES

- You will be able to dialogue about your college life such as how many classes you are taking, what kinds of classes you are taking, and the professors teaching the classes.
- You will be able to talk about how you like your current living place and introduce your roomate.
- You will be able to write about and present your college life or your friend's.

KEY EXPRESSIONS AND STRUCTURES

- 대학 생활이 어때요?: How's your college life?
- 이번 학기에 몇 과목 들어요?: How many classes are you taking this semester?
- 이번 학기에 무슨 수업 들어요?: What kind of classes are you taking?
- 한국어 가르치시는 선생님이 누구세요?: Who is the professor teaching your Korean class?

TASK: TALKING ABOUT YOUR COLLEGE LIFE

Talk about your college life, such as how many classes you are taking, what kind of classes you are taking, and the professors teaching the classes. Talk about your current home and introduce your roommate.

PRACTICE QUESTIONS

1. **대학 생활이 어때요?** 친구 많이 사귀었어요?
2. 이번 학기에 **몇 과목 들어요?**
3. 이번 학기에 **무슨 수업 들어요?**
4. 한국어 수업 듣는데 어때요?
5. 한국어 **가르치시는 선생님이 누구세요?**
6. 룸메이트도 인디애나 대학교 학생이에요?

ACTIVITY 1: 여러분의 대학 생활에 대해서 이야기 해 보세요.

Talk about your college life. Include the following things:

- How is your life in college?
- How many classes are you taking this semester?
- What kinds of classes are you taking this semester?
- Who are the professors teaching the classes?

[모델 대화]

제임스:	라일리 씨, **대학 생활이 어때요?**
라일리:	재미있는데 수업이 많아서 힘들어요.
제임스:	이번 학기에 **몇 과목 들어요?**
라일리:	다섯 과목 들어요.
제임스:	다섯 과목이나 들어요? 정말 힘들겠어요.
라일리:	네, 매일 수업이 있어서 정말 바빠요. 제임스 씨는요?
제임스:	저는 이번 학기에 두 과목 들어요.
라일리:	**무슨 수업 들어요?**
제임스:	한국어 수업하고 음악 수업을 들어요.
라일리:	이번 학기에 음악 **수업 가르치시는 선생님이 누구세요?**
제임스:	브라운 선생님이신데 아주 좋으세요.

_____

_____

_____

_____

ACTIVITY 2: 기숙사 생활과 룸메이트에 대해서 말해 보세요.

Talk to your partner about your current home and your roommate. Include the following things:

- Where you live
- How long you have been living there
- How you like it
- How many roommates you have
- Your roomate if you have one

[모델 대화]

라일리:	제임스 씨, 어디 살아요?
제임스:	기숙사에 살아요.
라일리:	**기숙사에서 얼마 동안 살았어요?**
제임스:	2년 동안 살았어요.
라일리:	**기숙사 생활이 어때요?**
제임스:	학교가 가까워서 좋은데 식당이 없어서 불편해요.
라일리:	룸메이트 있어요?
제임스:	네, 한 명 있어요.
라일리:	**룸메이트도 인디애나 대학교 학생이에요?**
제임스:	네, 저하고 한국어 수업을 같이 듣는데 아주 친절해요.

_____

_____

_____

_____

_____

ACTIVITY 3-1: 여러분 친구들의 대학 생활에 대해서 인터뷰해 보세요.

Interview two of your classmates about their college life and take notes in the table provided.

[Interview Questions]

1. 몇 학년이에요?
2. 어디 살아요?
3. 얼마 동안 _____에 살았어요?
4. 룸메이트 있어요? 몇 명 있어요?
5. 룸메이트도 인디애나 대학교 학생이에요?
6. 이번 학기에 몇 과목 들어요?
7. 무슨 수업 들어요?
8. _____ 수업 듣는데 어때요?
9. _____ 수업 가르치시는 선생님이 누구세요?

Interview Qs	친구 1: 김유진	친구 2:
1.	2 학년이에요	
2. 3.	기숙사에 살아요. 2 년동안 살았어요.	
4. 5.	룸메이트가 1 명 있어요. 네, 룸메이트 이름은 에밀리예요. 에밀리 씨도 2 학년이고, 경제학 전공해요.	
6. 7. 8. 9.	이번 학기에 5 과목 들어요 심리학, 수학, 경제학, 한국어 수업을 들어요. 심리학 수업은 재미있는데 어려워요. 선생님은 브라운 선생님이세요.	

ACTIVITY 3-1: 대학 생활에 대해 인터뷰한 내용을 발표해 보세요.

After the interview, present your classmate's college life to the class.

[모델 리포트]

유진 씨는 2 학년입니다. 지금 기숙사에 삽니다. 기숙사에서 2 년 동안 살았습니다. 룸메이트가 1 명 있는데 아주 친절합니다. 유진 씨 룸메이트 이름은 에밀리입니다. 에밀리 씨도 인디애나 대학교 2 학년입니다. 경제학을 전공합니다.

유진 씨는 이번 학기에 5 과목이나 듣습니다. 심리학, 수학, 경제학, 피아노, 그리고 한국어 수업을 듣습니다. 심리학 수업은 재미있는데 어렵습니다. 심리학을 가르치시는 선생님은 브라운 선생님이십니다.

_____

_____

_____

_____

_____

_____

WRAP-UP ACTIVITY

Write about your college life. Include where you live, how many classes and what kinds of classes you are taking this semester, the professors teaching the classes, and so forth.

[모델 작문]

저는 인디애나 대학교 1 학년입니다. 한국어를 전공합니다. 이번 학기에 4 과목을 듣습니다. 한국어 수업, 한국 문화 수업, 한국 역사 수업, 그리고 음악 수업을 듣습니다. 한국어 수업은 재미있는데 조금 어렵습니다. 한국어를 가르치시는 선생님은 김지영 선생님이십니다.

대학 생활이 아주 재미있습니다. 지금 기숙사에 삽니다. 기숙사에서 한 학기 동안 살았습니다. 룸메이트가 1 명 있는데 아주 좋습니다. 룸메이트 이름은 김수지입니다. 수지 씨도 인디애나 대학교 1 학년입니다. 이번 학기에 저하고 같이 한국어 수업을 듣습니다.

_____

_____

_____

_____

_____

_____

CULTURAL AWARENESS: WHAT IS THE SPECIAL CULTURE OF UNIVERSITIES IN KOREA? 엠티 (M.T.)

What is the special culture of universities in Korea? Have you heard of 엠티 (M.T.)? 엠티 looks like English, but it is actually Konglish (Korean + English). It is made up of English words (membership training) but it is used only in Korea. It is used to refer to a trip a member of an organization in college/university goes on.   Usually at the beginning of semester, they go to a suburb for 1 or 2 days. There are many kinds of 엠티 s: 과 엠티 (department M.T.), 동아리 엠티 (club M.T.), and so on. The activities students do during the 엠티 are usually for fun: playing soccer/badminton, playing group games, camping, and so forth. The most fun part is that they get to know the seniors in the same department or the club. So, if you are a freshman in a Korean university, 엠티 is a can't-miss event.

Figure 6.1 Hiking.

Credit

Fig. 6.1: Copyright © 2017 Pixabay/StockSnap.

CHAPTER 7. RESPONDING TO WHAT'S NEW IN LIFE
봄방학에 정말 재미있겠네요!

OBJECTIVES

- You will be able to make a comment on and respond to something you noticed/realized.
- You will be able to post a comment on the latest news on a friend's SNS.
- You will be able to have a conversation with a friend who you haven't seen for a long time about what's new with you.
- You will be able to write a text message and present it to the class.

KEY EXPRESSIONS AND STRUCTURES

- V/Adj. ~네요 (Sentence ender): Ending used when reacting to a new situation
- V/Adj. ~겠네요 (Sentence ender): I think you must be . . .
- 정말 좋겠네요!: You must be really happy!
- 봄 방학: Spring break, 댓글: reply, 안부: someone's regards, 인스타그램: Instagram

TASK: REACTING TO A NEW SITUATION

Visit a friend's Facebook/Instagram and post a comment on a recent post.

PRACTICE QUESTIONS

Give an appropriate response to the following situations by using ~겠네요.

1. 어제 2시간밖에 못 잤어요.
2. 한국어 시험에서 A+를 받았어요.
3. 오늘 저녁에 한국 식당에서 불고기를 먹을 거예요.
4. 수업이 많아서 점심을 못 먹었어요.
5. 봄 방학 때 플로리다에 가서 수영할 거예요.

ACTIVITY 1: 다음 그림을 보고 알게 된 것에 대해 말해 보세요.

Comment on what you notice from the following picture.

Figure 7.1 Lecture.

[예시]

1. 학생들이 아주 많**네요!**

2.

3.

4.

5.

…

ACTIVITY 2: 친구의 인스타그램에 올라온 사진에 댓글을 달아 보세요.

Comment on a classmate's Instagram.

[Instagram]

1.

Figure 7.2 Chicken soup

♥ #Korean#Food#chicken soup

[보기]   Jiyoungusa 삼계탕 먹었어요?

정말 맛있었겠네요!

2.

Figure 7.3 Cat

♥#MyPet#cat#kitty

3.

Figure 7.4 New York

♥#NewYork#tourist#manhattan

4.

Figure 7.5 Roses

♥#Flower Gift#birthday#Roses

ACTIVITY 3: 오랜만에 만난 친구와 안부를 묻고 친구의 새로운 소식에 반응해 보세요.

You run into a friend you haven't seen for a long time. Talk about how you have been doing and what's new with you. Comment on something you find new or surprising about your friend.

[모델 대화]

미나: 어머, 마크 씨 아니세요? 오랜만이에요.

마크: 네, 미나 씨! 오랜만이에요.

미나: 어떻게 지내세요?

마크: 잘 지내요. 저는 이번 학기에 졸업해요.

미나: 아, 그래요? 정말 **좋겠네요!**

마크: 미나 씨는 어떻게 지내세요?

미나: 저도 잘 지내요. 저는 이번 여름 방학에 한국에 가요.

            친구가 한국에 있는데 같이 여행 할 거예요.

마크: 그래요? 정말 **재미있겠네요!**

_____

_____

_____

_____

_____

_____

ACTIVITY 4: 반 친구들이 봄 방학에 한 일/ 할 일에 대해서 인터뷰하고 반응해 보세요.

Interview three classmates about plans for spring break. (If spring break already passed, talk about what you did during the break.)

[모델 대화]

미나:	마크 씨는 봄 방학에 뭐 할 거예요?
마크:	저는 친구하고 플로리다에 가서 수영할 거예요.
미나:	**와~ 재미있겠네요!**
마크:	미나 씨는 뭐 할 거예요?
미나:	저는 봄 방학 끝나고 시험이 2 개나 있어서 공부할 거예요.
마크:	그래요? 그럼 아주 **바쁘겠네요.**

이름	봄 방학에 한 일/할 일
마크	플로리다에서 수영할 거예요
미나	시험이 있어서 공부할 거예요
친구 1. _____	
친구 2. _____	
친구 3. _____	

WRAP-UP ACTIVITY

Write a text message to a friend you haven't seen for a long time with the latest news about yourself. Then, present it to the class.

[모델 작문]

수지 씨, 안녕하세요?

오랜만이에요. 잘 지내요?

저는 이번 학기에 졸업할 거예요. 그래서 이번 학기에 너무 바빠요. 5 과목이나 들어서 매일 수업이 있어요.

수지 씨는 어떻게 지내요? 이번 봄 방학에 뭐 할 거예요? 플로리다에 가서 수영 할 거예요? 정말 재미있겠네요!

_____

_____

_____

_____

_____

_____

_____

Cultural Awareness: KakaoTalk 카카오톡 메세지

KakaoTalk is a messenger service that allows you to send and receive messages for free anywhere in the world. Kakao Co., Ltd. launched and used the messenger app for the first time, and there is no Korean smartphone user who doesn't use this app. It is no exaggeration to say that KakaoTalk has created a new culture. New terms, expressions, and emoticons seem to have already entered our lives deeply and become part of daily life. There are many expressions created because a lot of abbreviations and acronyms are used in KakaoTalk. In particular, in Korean, consonants and vowels are combined into one syllable letter, so abbreviations are often made up of only consonants, such as ㅋㅋ and ㅎㅎ, which means laughter. When reducing sentences or phrases rather than one word, people often make abbreviations by taking the first letter of the word unit, such as 생파 reduced from 생일 파티 and 여친/남친 from 여자 친구/남자 친구. Teenagers and young generations use these new terms a lot, which sometimes causes difficulty in communication between generations. Considering the convenience of KakaoTalk, however, people are willing to bear the negative side.

Figure 7.6 KakaoTalk.

Credits

Fig. 7.1: Copyright © 2013 Pixabay/nikolayhg.
Fig. 7.2: Copyright © 2016 Pixabay/cegoh.
Fig. 7.3: Copyright © 2016 Pixabay/Pexels.
Fig. 7.4: Copyright © 2016 Pixabay/ahundt.
Fig. 7.5: Copyright © 2017 Pixabay/Gellinger.
Fig. 7.6: Copyright © by Jon Russell (CC by 2.0) at https://www.flickr.com/photos/jonrussell/39564882404/.

CHAPTER 8. EXPRESSING GRATITUDE
도와 주셔서 감사합니다.

OBJECTIVES

- You will be able to make a request to get help from others.
- You will be able to talk about what you did/have done for others as well as what others did/have done for you.
- You will be able to express your gratitude for things that others did for you.
- You will be able to write a thank-you card to a person you are grateful to.

KEY EXPRESSIONS AND STRUCTURES

- V ~어/아 주다 (Sentence ender): To do something for others.
- V ~어/아 주세요: Please V for me.
- V ~어/아 주셔서 감사합니다/고맙습니다: Thank you for V-ing for me.
- 도와 주셔서 감사합니다: Thank you for your help.
- 뭘 도와 줄까요?/드릴까요?: What can I help you?

TASK: SAY THANK YOU FOR WHAT PEOPLE DID FOR YOU

Ask a friend for help and then write a thank-you card to them.

PRACTICE QUESTIONS

1. 친구 생일에 뭐 **사 줬어요**?
2. 동생 생일에 선물 **사 줬어요**?
3. 어버이 날에 부모님께 뭐 **해 드렸어요**?
4. 룸메이트한테 뭘 **도와 줬어요**?
5. 제가 뭘 **도와 드릴까요**?

KEY PATTERN PRACTICE 1

Make a polite request for the following things by using ~어/아 주세요:

1. (To teacher) Speak slowly please.

   _____

2. (To taxi driver) Go to Seoul Station please.

   _____

3. (To roommate) Do the laundry please.

   _____

4. (To parents) Send me money please.

   _____

KEY PATTERN PRACTICE 2

Suppose that someone did the following things for you and you express your gratitude. Use the pattern ~어/아 주셔서 감사합니다:

1. Coming to your birthday party

   ___파티에 와 주셔서 감사합니다._____

2. Inviting you to Thanksgiving dinner

   _____

3. Calling you

   _____

4. Helping you with homework

   _____

5. Listening to your presentation

   _____

ACTIVITY 1: 다른 사람들에게 해 주거나 도와 준 것을 써 보세요.

Think about what you usually do/have done for others and write it out, as in the example. Then share your writing with the class.

[보기]

To whom	What you have done/helped:
형제	저는 자주 동생 숙제를 **도와 줍니다.**
룸메이트	룸메이트한테 저녁을 만들어 **주었습니다.**
(여자/남자) 친구	오늘 아침에 친구한테 커피를 **사 주었습니다.**
어머니/아버지	어머니 생신에 꽃을 **사 드렸습니다.**

To whom	What you have done/helped:
형제	
룸메이트	
(여자/남자) 친구	
어머니/아버지	

ACTIVITY 2: 친구에게 도움을 요청해 보세요.

Ask your friend for help in the following situations:

- Homework for Korean class
- Carrying a lot of heavy books
- Taking a picture of yourself
- Clean a kitchen at your dorm

[모델 대화]

미나:	마크 씨, 뭐 하세요?
마크:	한국어 숙제 하고 있는데 좀 어렵네요.
미나:	제가 **도와 줄까요?/드릴까요?**
마크:	네, 그럼 워크북 단어를 좀 찾**아 주세요.**
미나:	네, 제가 도**와 줄게요.**
마크:	**도와 주셔서 감사합니다!**

_____

_____

_____

_____

_____

_____

ACTIVITY 3: 다른 사람들의 도움이 필요하세요? 문자 메세지를 남겨 보세요.

Suppose that you need some help from the following people. Choose one of them and send a text message asking for help.

- 한국어 반 친구에게
- 룸메이트에게
- 어머니/아버지께
- 동생/언니/오빠/누나에게
- 선생님께 (이번 학기에 듣고 있는 수업)

[보기] 한국어 반 친구에게

To.

에밀리 씨, 안녕하세요?
저 김유진이에요.

어제 한국어 수업에 못
갔는데 숙제가 뭐예요?
숙제 좀 **가르쳐 주세요.**

Figure 8.1 Text messages.

WRAP-UP ACTIVITY

Write a thank-you card to someone you are grateful to, as in the sample. You may write to the person you received help from in Activity 2. Or you may write a card to your mother/father to celebrate the upcoming Mother's/Father's/Parents' Day. Then present your card to the class.

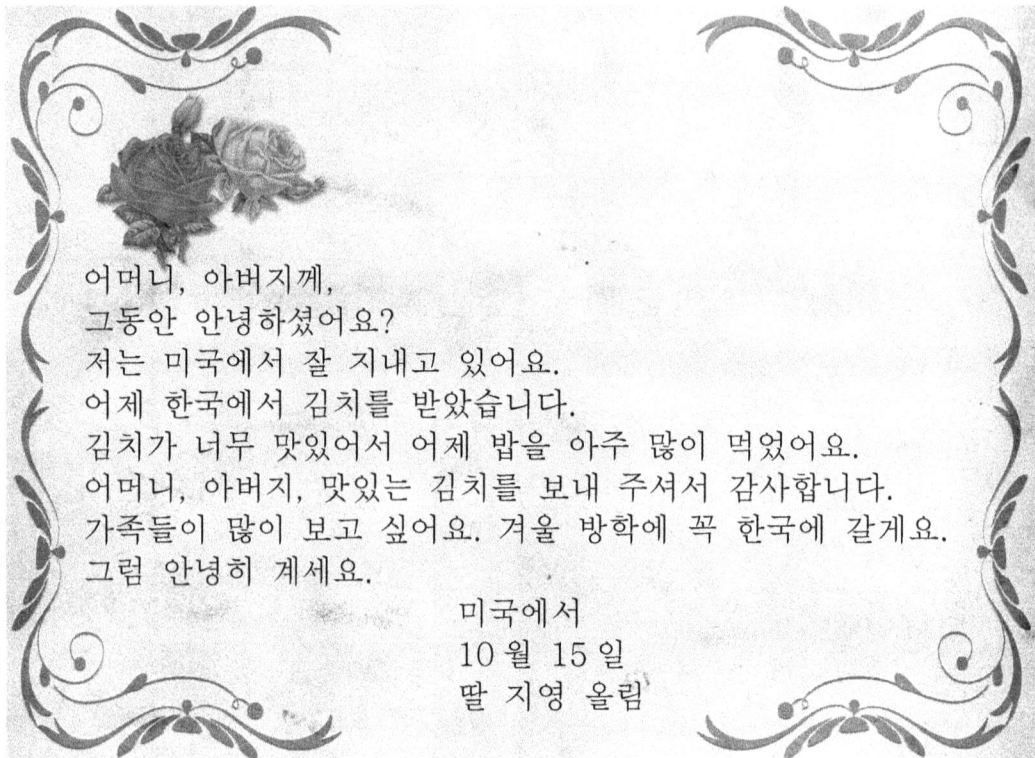

어머니, 아버지께,
그동안 안녕하셨어요?
저는 미국에서 잘 지내고 있어요.
어제 한국에서 김치를 받았습니다.
김치가 너무 맛있어서 어제 밥을 아주 많이 먹었어요.
어머니, 아버지, 맛있는 김치를 보내 주셔서 감사합니다.
가족들이 많이 보고 싶어요. 겨울 방학에 꼭 한국에 갈게요.
그럼 안녕히 계세요.
　　　　　　미국에서
　　　　　　10 월 15 일
　　　　　　딸 지영 올림

Figure 8.2a　[보기] Thank-you card.

Figure 8.2b Thank-you card.

_____

_____

_____

_____

_____

_____

_____

CULTURAL AWARENESS: PARENTS' DAY IN KOREA 한국의 어버이날

People observe May 8 as Parents' Day in Korea. Unlike America, where people celebrate two separate days, Mother's Day and Father's Day, a single day is designated for both mothers and fathers. One of the traditions on Parents' Day is for children to give their parents red carnations. This tradition started because the red carnation means gratitude, love, and respect. Around May 8 어버이날, every market sells bouquets and pots of the flowers. Some students make the flower themselves since some schools offer an opportunity for students to make an origami of the carnation in an art class.

In addition to the flower, many people give a gift to their parents. You will see a variety of gift sets at department stores and convenience stores on 어버이날. Some people visit their parents on May 8 by bringing the gift, and others send the gift via a delivery service. If you feel some burden of preparing a gift on 어버이날, just write a thank-you card. I am sure your parents will be very happy with the card you write.

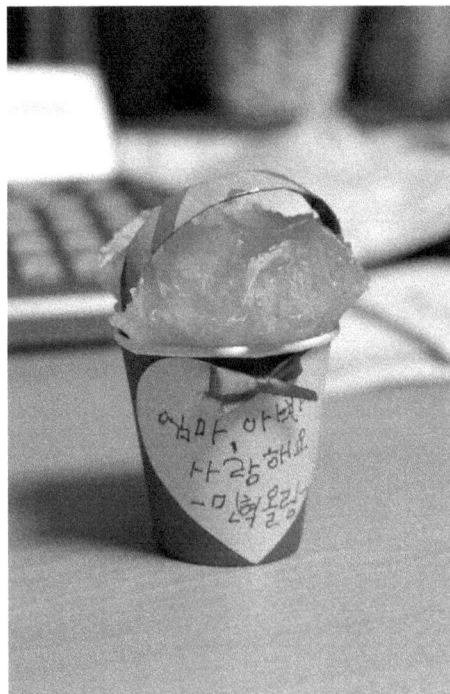

Figure 8.3 Carnation origami with a thank-you message.

Credits

CHAPTER 9. TALKING ABOUT THINGS TO DO
이번 주에 할 일이 많아요

OBJECTIVES

- You will be able to talk about things to do for the upcoming day/week.
- You will be able to describe your plans for a weekend by giving details about things to do, people to meet, places to visit, and so forth.
- You will be able to verbalize essential etiquettes to follow in public places such as a library, theater, airplane, and so on.
- You will be able to make suggestions of what to do when someone needs advice.
- You will be able to write about and present things to do in the upcoming day/week.

KEY EXPRESSIONS AND STRUCTURES

- V ~(어/아)야 돼요 (Sentence ender): Should/must/need to V
- V ~(으)ㄹ 것/일: Things to do/V
- V ~어/아야 될 것/일: Things you should do/V
- 어떻게 해야 될까요?: What should I do?

TASK: TALKING ABOUT THINGS TO DO FOR THE UPCOMING WEEK

Talk about things to do in the upcoming week by saying what you should do for classes this week. Give details about things to do, people to meet, and places to visit.

PRACTICE QUESTIONS

Ask the following questions about things to do today:

1. 오늘 **해야 할 일**이 뭐예요*?*
2. 오늘 **공부할 거** 많아요?
3. 오늘 도서관에서 **읽어야 될 책** 있어요?
4. 오늘 **만나야 할 사람** 있어요?
5. 오늘 룸메이트하고 마켓에서 **살 거** 많아요?

ACTIVITY 1: 다음 공공장소에서 꼭 지켜야 될 에티켓을 이야기해 보세요.

Talk about essential etiquette in the public places. You may use the words in the box.

[단어]

핸드폰 끄다: to turn off cellphone, 조용히 하다: to be quiet, 티켓을 사다: to buy a ticket, 안전벨트 하다: to fasten a seat belt , 열심히 공부하다: to study hard

---

장소 (Public places)	지켜야 될 에티켓 (Etiquettes to observe)
극장	1. 핸드폰을 **꺼야 돼요** 2. 3.
도서관	1. 2. 3.
비행기	1. 2. 3.

ACTIVITY 2: 다음과 같은 직업을 가지려면 어떻게 해야 될까요?

What qualifications are needed to get a job in the following pictures?

1.

Figure 9.1 Singer

2.

Figure 9.2 Chef

가수가 되고 싶으면, ___노래를 잘 **해야 돼요.**___	요리사가 되고 싶으면, _____

3.

Figure 9.3 Basketball Player

4.

Figure 9.4 Newscaster

농구 선수가 되고 싶으면, _____	아나운서가 되고 싶으면, _____

ACTIVITY 3: 이러한 상황에서는 어떻게 해야 될까요?

Talk about what you should do in the following situations. Take notes in the table provided.

- 한국어를 잘하고 싶은데 **어떻게 해야 될까요?**
- 한국어를 전공하고 싶은데 **어떻게 해야 돼요?**
- 피아노를 잘 치고 싶은데 **어떻게 해야 될까요?**
- 학교에서 다운타운까지 **어떻게 가야 돼요?**
- 겨울 방학에 한국에 여행 갈 거예요. 뭐 준비**해야 될까요?**

[보기]

1. A: 한국어를 잘하고 싶은데 **어떻게 해야 될까요?**

    B: 매일 한국어를 **연습해야 돼요.**

    그리고 한국 친구하고 자주 이야기해 보세요.

Situations	What to do
1. 한국어를 잘하고 싶어요.	매일 한국어를 **연습해야 돼요.**
2. 한국어를 전공하고 싶어요.	
3. 피아노를 잘 치고 싶어요.	
4. 학교에서 다운타운까지 가야 돼요.	
5. 겨울 방학에 한국에 여행 갈 거예요.	

ACTIVITY 4: 주말에 해야 될 일에 대해서 이야기 해 보세요.

Suppose that you have a lot of things to do this weekend, as in the following situations. Talk to your partner about things to do.

- Things to buy at a market: milk, juice, apples, and so forth
- Subjects to study: Korean, Korean literature, economics, and so forth
- People to meet: a friend, a classmate, and so forth
- Places to go to: parents' place, library, lab, and so forth

[모델 대화]

유진: 수지 씨, 이번 주말에 **할 일** 많으세요?

수지: 네, 많아요. 한국어 숙제도 **해야 되고** 경제학 페이퍼도 **써야 돼요.**

  유진 씨는 주말에 **뭐 해야 돼요?**

유진: 저도 이번 주말에 **공부할 거** 많아요.

  한국 문학 책도 읽**어야 되고** 경제학 숙제도 **해야 돼요.**

수지: 네, 그럼 주말 잘 보내세요!

유진: 네, 수지 씨도 주말 잘 보내세요!

_____

_____

_____

_____

_____

_____

_____

Wrap-Up Activity

Write about things to do next week. You may summarize what you talked about in Activity 1.
Then present your writing to the class.

[모델 작문]

저는 다음 주에 할 일이 많아서 좀 바쁠거예요. 월요일에 한국어 시험이 있어서
시험 준비를 해야 돼요. 화요일에는 수학 숙제를 해야 되고 수요일에는 경제학
레포트도 써야 돼요. 목요일에는 숙제가 없어요. 금요일에 오전에는 한국어 선생님
오피스 아워에 가서 한국어 연습해야 되고, 오후에는 KCC 미팅에 가야 돼요.

_____

_____

_____

_____

_____

_____

_____

_____

_____

CULTURAL AWARENESS: BEST JOBS FOR COLLEGE STUDENTS IN KOREA
한국 학생들이 선호하는 직업

The jobs Korean students prefer and those American students prefer are very different. The top five preferred jobs in Korea these days are teachers/professors, civil servants, employees of large companies, doctors/dentists, and entertainers. The popularity of teachers and civil servants always ranks high in Korea because people consider the income and stability of the job. In Korea, you must pass the National Teachers' Exam in order to become a teacher, which is very competitive—well above the average of 10 to 1 every year. In Korea, teachers are the most preferred jobs, especially among women, because they are guaranteed job stability and also have vacations.

As Korean people's perception changes, however, their preferred jobs seem to change little by little with the times. Since the 2000s, with the rapid development of technology, Koreans' preferred jobs have also changed. For example, due to the recent global popularity of K-pop, more students want to become idols, and more students want to become stars or influencers through YouTube.

Figure 9.5 Jobs.

Credits

CHAPTER 10. TALKING ABOUT DO'S AND DON'TS
수업 시간에 핸드폰 하지 마세요!

OBJECTIVES

- You will be able to talk about the do's and don'ts in public places such as a library, classroom, and movie theater.
- You will be able to give advice and suggest solutions on someone's problems and concerns.
- You will be able to discuss the difference in etiquette between Korean and American cultures.
- You will be able to write about and present your problems and concerns, including possible solutions.

KEY EXPRESSIONS AND STRUCTURES

- V ~(으)세요: Please do sth. (Polite command)
- V ~지 마세요: Don't do sth.
- V1 ~지 말고 V2 ~(으)세요: Don't V1 but V2.
- V ~(어/아)야 돼요 (Sentence ender): Should/must/need to V
- 어떻게 해야 돼요?: What should I do?
- 어떻게 해야 될까요? What do you think I should do?

TASK: TALKING ABOUT DO'S AND DON'TS IN DIFFERENT SITUATIONS

Make classroom rules in your Korean class and talk about common rules to follow in public places and different cultures.

PRACTICE QUESTIONS

1. 한국어를 잘 하고 싶은데 **어떻게 해야 돼요?**
2. 매일 수업에 늦는데 **어떻게 해야 될까요?**

KEY PATTERN PRACTICE

With your partner, talk about what the following symbols mean. Use the pattern ~지 마세요.

1. __전화를 하지 마세요___   2. _____   3. _____

4. _____   5. _____   3. _____

ACTIVITY 1: 다음 장소에서 지켜야 할 규칙에 대해 말해 봅시다.

Talk about do's and don'ts at the following places: library, classroom, and movie theatre.

도서관	한국어 교실	극장
조용히 **해야 돼요.**	영어를 쓰**지 마세요.**	
떠들**지 마세요.**		

ACTIVITY 2. 룸메이트와 하우스 룰을 만들어 보세요.

Suppose that you have rommates and make house rules for all to follow.

Negative commands (don'ts: ~지 마세요)	Positive commands (do's: ~(으)세요)
1. 늦게 일어나**지 마세요**.	1. 일찍 일어나세요.
2. 샤워는 밤에 하**지 마세요**.	2. 샤워는 아침에 하세요.
3.	3. 집에 일찍 오세요.
4.	4. 매일 청소하세요.
5.	5. 밤에 조용히 하세요
6.	6. 렌트비는 일찍 내세요.
7.	7. (Make up your own rule)

HOUSE RULES
1. 늦게 일어나**지 말고** 일찍 **일어나세요**.
2. 샤워는 밤에 하**지 말고** 아침에 **하세요**.
3.
4.
5.
6.
7. (Make up your own rule)

ACTIVITY 3: 미국과 한국 문화를 비교하여 각 나라에서 지켜야 할 예절이나 문화에 대해서 이야기 해 봅시다.

Discuss the difference between Kore and your country. Are there any etiquette rules or manners in Korean culture that are different from your country? Take notes in the table and present it to the class.

한국에서는	미국에서는 (or your home country)
어른들께 존댓말을 **써야 돼요.**	서버한테 팁을 **줘야 돼요.**
집 안에서 신발을 신**지 마세요.**	나이를 물어 보**지 마세요.**

_____

_____

_____

_____

_____

_____

ACTIVITY 4: 반 친구들의 고민을 해결 해 주세요.

Consult your partner about concerns and problems you have. Give advice and suggest some solutions, as in the examples provided.

[보기 1]

A: 한국어를 잘 하고 싶은데 **어떻게 해야 돼요?**

B: 수업 시간에 영어를 하**지 말고** 한국어만 **하세요.**

   그리고 한국 드라마를 많이 **보세요.**

[보기 2]

A: 매일 수업에 늦는데 **어떻게 해야 될까요?**

B: 밤에 늦게 자**지 말고** 일찍 **자세요.**

고민들 (Problems)	해결책 (Possible solutions)
한국어를 잘 하고 싶어요.	
매일 수업에 늦어요.	
건강이 안 좋아요.	
핸드폰을 너무 많이 해요.	
룸메이트하고 사이가 안 좋아요.	

WRAP-UP ACTIVITY

Write about concerns and problems you have. You may write about the problem you talked about in Activity 4. Include possible solutions and advice you got from someone. Then present it to the class.

[모델 작문]

저는 한국어를 배우는데 좀 어려워요. 한국어를 매일 연습해야 돼요. 수업 시간에 영어를 하지 말고 한국어만 해야 돼요. 한국 친구도 많이 만나야 돼요. 한국 드라마도 많이 봐야 돼요. 그리고 한국어 선생님 오피스 아워에 자주 가서 연습해야 돼요.

_____

_____

_____

_____

_____

_____

_____

_____

CULTURAL AWARENESS: KOREAN SUPERSTITIONS 한국의 미신

Each country and each culture has interesting superstitions. Let me introduce what kind of superstitions that Koreans believe in.

1. 시험 보는 날 미역국을 먹지 마세요: Do not eat seaweed soup on an exam day.

This superstition is the most popular in Korea. It originated because the slippery texture of seaweed gives the idea of failing a test.

2. 여자 친구나 남자 친구에게 신발을 선물 하지 마세요: Do not buy shoes for your girlfriend or boyfriend.

If you give shoes to your girlfriend or boyfriend, they will go far away in those shoes.

3. 빨간 색으로 이름을 쓰지 마세요: Do not write a name in red.

Koreans never write their names in red because a dead person's name is written in red at the funeral.

4. 연인과 덕수궁 돌담길을 걷지 마세요: Do not walk with a lover along the Deoksugung Stonewall Walkway.

Deoksugung Stonewall Walkway (덕수궁 돌담길) in Korea is very famous for its beauty, but it is said that if you walk along the walkway with your lover, you will break up. Considering that 덕수궁 is a very famous place, many couples must have come on a date walking along the walkway, and there must have been many couples who have broken up.

5. 선풍기를 틀어 놓고 자지 마세요: Do not sleep with a fan on.

This is not scientifically true, so I think it's just a real superstition.

Credits

CHAPTER 11. ASKING FOR HELP AND FAVORS
한국어 숙제 좀 도와 줄 수 있어요?

OBJECTIVES

- You will be able to talk about what you can do such as speak foreign languages, play musical instruments, cook, and play sports.
- You will be able to discuss and present what kinds of activities are available in different cities/countries.
- You will be able to ask for help and offer favors to friends, professors, parents, and roommates.

KEY EXPRESSIONS AND STRUCTURES

- V ~(으)ㄹ 수 있다 (Sentence ender): can/to be able to V/it is possible to V
- V ~어/아 줄 수 있어요?: Could you please V for me?
- 도와 줄 수 있어요?: Can you please help me?
- 외국어: foreign language, 악기: musical instrument, 요리: cooking

TASK: TALKING ABOUT POSSIBILITIES AND ASKING FOR HELP

Talk about things you can do and ask for help from friends, professors, parents, and roommates.

PRACTICE QUESTIONS

1. 어떤 외국어를 **할 수 있어요?**
2. 어떤 한국 음식을 **만들 수 있어요?**
3. 내일 유진 씨 생일인데 파티에 **올 수 있어요?**
4. 이 책 좀 **빌려 줄 수 있어요?**
5. 한국어 숙제 좀 **도와 줄 수 있어요?**

ACTIVITY 1: 반 친구들이 잘 할 수 있는 외국어, 악기, 스포츠 그리고 잘 만들 수 있는 음식을 인터뷰해 보세요.

Interview three classmates about what they can do, such as speak foreign languages, play musical instruments, cook, and play sports.

[보기]

수지: 유진 씨, 어떤 <u>외국어</u>를 **할 수 있어요**?

유진: 한국어하고 일본어를 **할 수 있어요.**

　　　수지 씨는요?

수지: 저는 한국어밖에 못 해요.

	친구 1. 김유진	친구 2.	친구 3.
외국어	일본어		
스포츠	수영		
악기 (MUSICAL INSTRUMENT)	피아노		
요리 (COOKING)	비빔밥, 파스타		

[리포트]

유진 씨는 일본어를 할 수 있어요. 그리고 수영 할 수 있어요. 그리고 피아노 칠 수 있어요. 그리고 비빔밥하고 파스타를 만들 수 있어요.

ACTIVITY 2: 선생님, 부모님, 그리고 룸메이트한테 부탁해 보세요.

Suppose you have some favors to ask of your Korean professor, your parents, and your roommate. You can use the pattern ~어/아 줄 수 있으세요 when requesting. Write in the table.

ASK WHOM?	FAVOR TO ASK
한국어 선생님	1. 영어로 **말해 줄 수 있으세요?** 2. 3.
부모님 (어머니/아버지)	1. 돈 좀 부쳐 **줄 수 있으세요?** 2. 3.
룸메이트	1. 오늘 청소 좀 **해 줄 수 있어요?** 2. 3.

ACTIVITY 3: 친구에게 부탁이나 도움을 요청해 보세요.

Suppose that you are in the following situations. Ask a friend for help.

- Ask a friend to do homework together at a library.

- Ask a roommate to clean a house.

- Ask a friend to carry books to a professor's office.

- Ask a friend to go grocery shopping together.

[모델 대화]

수지: 유진 씨, 오늘 시간 있으세요?

유진: 네, 괜찮아요.

수지: 도서관에서 한국어 숙제 **같이 할 수 있어요?**

유진: 네, 같이 해요.

수지: 고마워요!

_____

_____

_____

_____

_____

_____

WRAP-UP ACTIVITY

Make a group of four students and talk about what kind of activities you can do in the following cities/countries. When done, choose one of them and present it to the class.

[장소]

디즈니랜드, 한국, 일본, 중국, 하와이, 뉴욕, 로스 앤젤레스, 시카고, 플로리다

[보기]

학생 1: 디즈니랜드에 가서 **뭘 할 수 있어요?**

학생 2: 미키 마우스하고 미니 마우스를 **만날 수 있어요.**

학생 3: 밤에는 불꽃 놀이도 **볼 수 있어요.**

학생 4: 아름다운 성(castle) 앞에서 사진도 **찍을 수 있어요.**

_____

_____

_____

_____

_____

_____

_____

CULTURAL AWARENESS: ARTS, MUSIC, AND PHYSICAL EDUCATION IN KOREA
한국의 예체능 교육

It is well known that Koreans are passionate about children's education. Their high passion for arts and sports education is no exception. A lot of Korean students start early, such as in elementary school, to attend institutes or receive private lessons for arts and sports education. Perhaps due to the passion for education, more Korean students have recently been recognized on the international stage. For instance, a figure skater, Kim Yu-na, won a gold medal in the 2010 Winter Olympics, and a pianist, Cho Sung-jin, won the grand prize at the 2015 International Chopin Competition for the first time among Koreans. And in many golf events, South Korean female students were ranked at the top for world-class championships.

In Korea, you can find a lot of piano and violin private academies in residential areas. And the number of sports-related academies has recently increased. It is expected that more world-class Korean athletes and musicians can be produced in the field of arts and sports in the future.

Figure 11.1 Yu-Na Kim.

Credit

CHAPTER 12. PURCHASING ITEMS AT A STORE
이거 하나에 얼마예요?

OBJECTIVES

- You will be able to say the price of items per unit.
- You will be able to ask questions to a clerk at a store.
- You will be able to talk about a shopping place.
- You will be able to write about and present your favorite shopping place and your shopping experience.

KEY EXPRESSIONS AND STRUCTURES

- 어서 오세요!: Welcome!
- 사이즈가 어떻게 되세요?/ 몇 사이즈 입으세요?: What's your size?
- 입어 보세요/신어 보세요: Try this on.
- ~에: per, for (e.g. 2 개에 5 달러예요: It is two for 5 dollars.)
- 마음에 들어요: I like it.
- 뭐 찾으세요?: What are you looking for?
- 다른 색도 있어요?: Do you have other colors?

TASK: PURCHASING ITEMS AT A STORE

Go to a shopping mall and ask a clerk questions about the price, size, and color of the item you like.

PRACTICE QUESTIONS

Ask and answer the following questions:

1. **신발/옷 사이즈가 어떻게 되세요?**
2. 몇 사이즈 입으세요?/신으세요?
3. 이거 **한번 입어 보시겠어요?**
4. 어떤 신발/옷을 찾으세요?
5. 이거 **다른 색도 있어요?**

ACTIVITY 1: 슈퍼마켓 전단지를 보고 가격을 말해 보세요.

Say the price of the food on a flyer of a grocery store.

[보기]

손님: 저기요, <u>치리오스</u> 얼마예요?

직원: 지금 세일이라서 <u>세 개에 9 달러</u>예요.

손님: 와, 싸네요!

<서울 슈퍼>

Figure 12.1 Cheerios

Figure 12.2 Jello

Figure 12.3 Cereal

Figure 12.4 Milk

Figure 12.5 Bread

Figure 12.6 Chocolate

ACTIVITY 2: 옷 가게에 가서 점원과 대화하고 옷을 사 보세요.

Have a conversation, with one student as a customer and one as a salesman at a clothing store.

[모델 대화]

점원: 어서 오세요. 뭘 도와 드릴까요?

유미: 청바지를 사러 왔는데요.

점원: 이 청바지 어때요? 요즘 [13]유행하는 청바지예요.

유미: 네, 이 스타일 괜찮네요. 색깔도 예뻐요.

점원: **한번 입어 보세요. 몇 사이즈 입으세요?**

유미: 스몰 사이즈 입어요.

점원: 네, 여기 있어요. 피팅룸은 저쪽에 있어요.

점원: (After a while) **마음에 드세요?**

유미: 네, 아주 **마음에 들어요.** 얼마예요?

점원: 지금 30% 세일해서 4 만 5 천원이에요.

유미: 그럼 이거 주세요.

_____

_____

_____

_____

_____

---

[13] 유행하다: to be in fashion

ACTIVITY 3: 신발 가게에 가 보세요.

Have a conversation, with one student as a customer and one as a salesman at a shoe store.

[모델 대화]

점원:　　　　어서 오세요. **어떤 신발을 찾으세요?**

유미:　　　　겨울 부츠를 찾는데요.

점원:　　　　네, 이게 요즘 많이 신는 부츠예요.

유미:　　　　**다른 색도 있어요?**

점원:　　　　네, 까만색하고 회색도 있어요.

유미:　　　　까만색 **한번 신어 볼게요.**

점원:　　　　**사이즈가 어떻게 되세요?**

유미:　　　　240 이에요. 이 부츠도 세일이에요?.

점원:　　　　네, 세일해서 5 만원이에요.

_____

_____

_____

_____

_____

_____

_____

ACTIVITY 4: 좋아하는 쇼핑 장소에 대해서 인터뷰해 보세요.

Interview two classmates about somewhere they often shop.

[인터뷰 질문]

1. 쇼핑하러 보통 어디 가세요?/ 보통 어디서 쇼핑하세요?/ 쇼핑하러 자주 가는 곳이 어디예요? (_____)
2. _____은/는 어디에 있어요?
3. _____에 얼마나 자주 가요?
4. _____에 왜 자주 가요?
5. _____은/는 몇 시에 문을 열어요?
6. _____에 언제 갔어요? 가서 뭐 샀어요?

	김유진	친구 1.	친구 2.
1.	칼리지 몰		
2.	다운타운		
3.	한달에 한번		
4.	값이 싸고 물건이 많아서		
5.	오전 10 시		
6.	지난주, 신발		

Wrap-Up Activity

Write about some where you often shop. Try to remember the last time you went there. Write about where it is, how often you go there, why you like it, what time it usually opens, what kind of things you purchased last time, and so forth.   You may simply answer the interview questions in Activity 6. After writing, present your favorite place to shop to the class.

[모델 작문]

저는 쇼핑하러 칼리지 몰에 자주 가요. 다운타운에 있는데 값이 싸고 물건이 많아서 자주 가요. 오전 10 시에 문을 열어요. 지난 주말에 수지하고 같이 칼리지 몰에 갔어요. 신발을 사러 갔어요. 까만색 부츠를 샀어요. 요즘 유행하는 스타일이라서 아주 마음에 들었어요. 세일해서 한켤레에 5 만원에 샀어요. 수지는 요즘 유행하는 청바지를 샀어요. 청바지도 세일해서 싸게 샀어요.

CULTURAL AWARENESS: TV HOME SHOPPING IN KOREA 한국 TV 홈쇼핑

Online shopping is more popular these days than offline shopping. I'm sure there's no one among you who hasn't bought something from Amazon. More people are enjoying online shopping in Korea as well. As evidence, there were only a few TV home shopping channels in the early 2000s, but the number is now countless. The first reason for using TV home shopping is the price. This is because they sell products in bulk, so they can be purchased at a much lower price than offline stores. Home shopping sales have been up since then, and each year records a new high. In order to attract more and more viewers and customers, celebrities often act as shopping hosts or appear on home shopping channels to introduce products.

Along with the increase in home shopping in Korea, the delivery industry has increased as well. The number of courier companies has also increased exponentially, and the number of people who specialize in courier services has also increased. Couriers delivering boxes on the streets of Korea are now very common. And the delivery of a parcel box in front of the house is a very common sight to see at any house every day.

Figure 12.7 Delivery man

Credits

CHAPTER 13. ORDERING FOOD IN A RESTAURANT

뭐 먹을래요?

OBJECTIVES

- You will be able to recommend to a dish that you've tasted before.
- You will be able to ask questions to decide what to eat in a restaurant.
- You will be able to order food from a waiter/waitress in a restaurant.
- You will be able to request a server to bring more food/water.
- You will be able to write about and present your favorite food and restaurant.

KEY EXPRESSIONS AND STRUCTURES

- V ~(으)ㄹ 래요 (Sentence ender): I intend to V.
- V ~어/아 보다 (Sentence ender): try doing something
- 뭐 먹을래요?: What would you like to eat?
- 뭐 드시겠어요?: What would you like to eat? (honorific)
- 한번 먹어 보세요: Try this dish.
- N 좀 더 주시겠어요?: Please get me some more N.

TASK: ORDERING FOOD IN A RESTAURANT

Go to a Korean restaurant with a friend and decide on what to eat. Suggest to the friend a delicious dish that you've tasted before.

PRACTICE QUESTIONS

Ask and answer the following questions.

1. 점심에 **뭐 먹을래요?**
2. **뭐 드시겠어요?**
3. 오늘은 불고기 **먹어 볼까요?**
4. 이모 식당에서 순두부 찌개 **먹어 봤어요?**
5. 서울 식당 김치 찌개가 맛있는데 저하고 같이 **가 볼래요?**

ACTIVITY 1: 맛있는 한국 음식을 추천해 주세요.

Suppose that you take a friend who has not eaten Korean food before to a Korean restaurant. Recommend a delicious Korean dish on the menu to your friend.

[보기]

A: OO 씨, ＿＿＿＿＿＿＿ 먹어 봤어요?

B: 아니요. 안 먹어 봤는데요.

A: 그럼, 한 번 먹어 보세요. 아주 맛있어요.

<한국 식당 메뉴>

1. 김치 볶음밥

Figure 13.1 Kimchi Fried Rice

2. 비빔밥

Figure 13.2 Rice mixed with vegetables and beef

3. 삼겹살

Figure 13.3 Pork Bacon

4. 냉면

Figure 13.4 Cold Noodles

5. 김밥

Figure 13.5 Seaweed roll

6. 떡볶이

Figure 13.6 Spicy Rice Cake

ACTIVITY 2: 한국 식당에 가 봅시다! (PART 1)

Go to a Korean restaurant with a friend and decide on something to eat by asking each other what you like. You may suggest a delicious dish that you've tasted before in the restaurant.

[모델 대화]

종업원: 어서 오세요. 몇 분이세요?

마크: 두 명인데요.

종업원: 네, 여기 앉으세요.

마크: 네, 감사합니다.

미나: 마크 씨, **뭐 먹을래요?**

마크: 글쎄요. 뭐가 맛있어요?

미나: 저는 여기서 비빔밥하고 된장찌개 **먹어 봤는데** 아주 맛있어요.

마크: 그래요? 그럼 비빔밥 한 번 먹어 볼게요.

미나: 네, 그럼 저는 된장찌개 먹을래요.

_____

_____

_____

_____

_____

_____

ACTIVITY 3: 한국 식당에 가 봅시다! (PART 2)

After deciding on an item, talk to a waiter/waitress about ordering food, as in the sample dialogue.

[모델 대화]

종업원:	**뭐 드시겠어요?**
미나:	저는 된장찌개 주세요.
종업원:	손님은요?
마크:	저는 비빔밥 먹을게요.
종업원:	네, 알겠습니다. 음료수는 뭐 갖다 드릴까요?
미나:	저는 따뜻한 물 주세요.
마크:	저는 콜라 마실게요.

_____

_____

_____

_____

_____

_____

_____

ACTIVITY 4: 한국 식당에 가 봅시다! (PART 3)

While eating, check to see if your friend like the dishes you ordered. You may recommend another delicious dish to your friend for the next time.

[모델 대화]

미나:	마크 씨, 비빔밥 **맛이 어때요?**
마크:	고추장을 많이 넣어서 좀 맵지만 맛있어요.
미나:	매운 음식 좋아하세요?
마크:	네, 좋아해요.
미나:	그럼 다음에는 김치 찌개를 **먹어 보세요.**
	조금 맵지만 아주 맛있을 거예요.
마크:	네, 다음에 한 번 **먹어 볼게요.**

_____

_____

_____

_____

_____

_____

_____

ACTIVITY 5: 한국 식당에 가 봅시다! (PART 4)

Order more food from the waiter/waitress. You may ask the waiter or waitress to bring more water as well.

[모델 대화]

미나:	여기 식당 반찬이 정말 맛있네요!
마크:	네, 김치가 참 맛있네요.
미나:	여기요!
종업원:	네, 뭐 더 갖다 드릴까요?
미나:	여기 반찬 **좀 더 주시겠어요?**
종업원:	네, 알겠습니다.
마크:	저는 물 좀 더 갖다 주세요.
종업원:	네, 알겠습니다. 금방 갖다 드릴게요.

_____

_____

_____

_____

_____

_____

ACTIVITY 6: 좋아하는 음식과 식당에 대해서 인터뷰해 보세요.

Interview two classmates about their favorite food and restaurant. Take note of it in the table.

[인터뷰 질문]

1. 제일 좋아하는 음식은 뭐예요? (ㅇㅇ)
2. ㅇㅇ은/는 맛이 어때요?
3. 어느 식당 ㅇㅇ이/가 제일 맛있어요?
4. 그 식당에 언제 갔어요? 누구하고 갔어요?
5. 음식 값은 얼마 나왔어요?
6. 언제 또 갈 거예요?

	김유진	친구 1.	친구 2.
1.	김치 볶음밥		
2.	맵지만 맛있어요		
3.	이모 식당		
4.	지난 주에 룸메이트하고		
5.	9 천원		
6.	다음 주말		

WRAP-UP ACTIVITY

Write about your favorite food and restaurant. Try to remember the last time you went. Write what your favorite food is, what it tastes like, with whom you went, how much you paid for the dish, and so forth. You may also answer the interview questions in Activity 6. After writing, present your favorite food and restaurant to the class.

[모델 작문]

저는 김치 볶음밥을 제일 좋아해요. 김치 볶음밥은 조금 맵지만 맛있어요. 학교 앞 이모 식당 김치 볶음밥이 제일 맛있어요. 저는 자주 이모 식당에 가요. 지난 주에는 룸메이트하고 이모 식당에 갔어요. 저는 김치 볶음밥을 먹고, 룸메이트는 비빔밥을 먹었어요. 음식 값은 9 천원이 나왔어요. 다음에는 이모 식당에서 불고기를 먹어 보고 싶어요.

CULTURAL AWARENESS: TABLE MANNERS IN KOREA 한국의 식사 예절

It is well known that Korean table manners are very strict; there are many rules to follow and not to follow. Especially when eating with elders including your parents and grandparents, there are many things to be careful about, so I hope you learn the table manners in advance before going to Korea.

These are the most basic table manners that you should keep in mind:

1. Wait until the elders start to eat.

2. Don't leave your seat during meals, and keep pace with your eating until the elders finish eating.

3. Do not eat by holding bowls; keep the bowls on the table.

4. Use a spoon to eat rice and soup, and chopsticks to eat side dishes.

5. Do not hold a spoon and chopsticks together in one hand.

6. Do not eat foods with your hands.

7. Don't rummage through foods with a spoon or chopsticks.

Among these, the most important are that you should not eat before the elders start eating, so please keep that in mind when eating with Koreans. If you observe at least this rule, you won't be considered rude.

Figure 13.7 Family dinner table

Credits

CHAPTER 14. TALKING ABOUT TRAVEL EXPERIENCES
한국에 가 봤어요?

OBJECTIVES

- You will be able to ask if someone has experience in trying diverse activities.
- You will be able to talk about travel experiences by saying which cities you traveled to, when, what activities you did, and so on.
- You will be able to talk about a city/country that you wish to travel in the future.
- You will be able to write about and present your travel experiences to the class.

KEY EXPRESSIONS AND STRUCTURES

- V ~어/아 보다 (Sentence ender): Try doing something.
- V ~어/아 봤어요?: Have you ever tried V-ing?
- N 에 가 봤어요?: Have you been to N?
- N 해 보고 싶어요: I wish to try N.

TASK: TALKING ABOUT YOUR TRAVEL EXPERIENCE

Talk about your experience traveling to different countries and cities, including what activities you've tried. Discuss travel spots you wish to travel to in the future and what activities you wish to try there.

KEY PATTERN PRACTICE

Ask and answer the following questions:

1. 시카고에 **가 봤어요?**

2. 떡볶이 먹**어 봤어요?**

3. 스카이 다이빙 **해 봤어요?**

4. BTS 노래 들**어 봤어요?**

5. 지하철 **타 봤어요?**

ACTIVITY 1: 반 친구들은 어떤 경험을 해 봤는지 알아 보세요.

Interview your classmates and find out who has experienced and not experienced the following things. Write names in the table and find who has the most diverse experience.

[보기 1]

A: OO 씨, 한국에 **가 봤어요?**

B: 네, **가 봤어요.**

[보기 2]

A: OO 씨, 스노우 보드 **타 봤어요?**

B: 아니요, **안 타 봤는데** 한번 **타 보고 싶어요.**

경험 (Experiences)	이름
한국에 가 본 사람	유진
뉴욕에 가 본 사람	
스노우보드 타 본 사람	
번지 점프 해 본 사람	
워터파크에 가 본 사람	
K-pop 콘서트에 가 본 사람	
떡볶이 먹어 본 사람	
한복 입어 본 사람	

ACTIVITY 2: 여행한 곳에 대해서 이야기 해 봅시다.

Talk about your (overseas) travel experiences. Include which countries/cities you traveled, when, what activities you did/didn't do, and so forth.

[모델 대화]

데이빗: 에밀리 씨는 외국에 **가 봤어요?**

에밀리: 네, 한국에 **가 봤어요.**

데이빗: 언제 **가 봤어요?**

에밀리: 지난 여름에 갔는데 정말 재미 있었어요.

데이빗: 한국에서 어느 도시에 **가 봤어요?**

에밀리: 서울을 여행했는데 정말 크고 사람도 많았어요.

데이빗: 남산에서 케이블카도 **타 봤어요?**

에밀리: 아니요. 남산에는 못 갔어요.

데이빗: 저는 한국에서 남산 케이블카를 **타 보고 싶어요.**

ACTIVITY 3: 여행 가 보고 싶은 곳에 대해서 이야기 해 보세요.

Talk about a city/country you wish to travel to in the future. Include what you wish to do when you travel there.

[모델 대화]

에밀리: 데이빗 씨, 방학에 하고 싶은 것 있어요?

데이빗: 저는 한국을 **여행 해 보고 싶어요.**

에밀리: 한국에서 뭐 하고 싶은데요?

데이빗: 경복궁에 가서 한복도 **입어 보고 싶고,** 홍대 앞도 **가 보고 싶어요.**

           에밀리 씨는 방학에 **뭐 해 보고 싶어요?**

에밀리: 저는 유럽을 **여행 해 보고 싶어요.**

데이빗: 아 그래요?

에밀리: 유럽에 있는 많은 나라에 다 **가 보고 싶어요**

데이빗: 유럽에 가면 정말 재미있겠네요!

_____

_____

_____

_____

_____

_____

_____

WRAP-UP ACTIVITY

Write about your (overseas) travel experiences based on what you talked about in Activity 2. Include which countries/cities you traveled, when, what activities you did/didn't do, and so forth. Then present it to the class.

[모델 작문]

저는 한국에 가 봤어요. 지난 여름에 갔는데 정말 재미있었어요. 한국에서 서울을 여행했어요. 서울은 정말 크고 사람도 많았어요. 경복궁하고 덕수궁도 갔어요. 사진을 많이 찍었어요. 남산에 가서 서울 타워도 봤어요. 제주도에 가고 싶었지만 못 갔어요. 다음에는 제주도에 가 보고 싶어요.

_____

_____

_____

_____

_____

_____

_____

_____

_____

CULTURAL AWARENESS: TOURIST ATTRACTIONS IN KOREA 한국의 관광지

There are many tourist attractions in Korea that many foreigners visit. Among them, Jongno-gu of Seoul, where Gyeongbok Palace (경복궁) and Deoksu Palace (덕수궁) are located, is the most visited place because you can feel the tradition of Korea, and it has modern Korean cultures as well. Also there is Gwanghwamun Square (광화문 광장) in Jongno-gu, which is a symbol of Korean democracy that attracts tourists. Recently, the number of foreign tourists visiting Korea has increased, and accordingly many events and services can be seen to experience and enjoy Korean traditions. When entering Gyeongbok Palace, for example, tourists wearing 한복 (Korean traditional dress) can enter for free, and various events such as tasting Korean foods for foreigners can also be enjoyed. Foreigners wearing 한복 on Jongno-gu Street are no longer unfamiliar.

If you travel outside of Seoul in Korea, Jeju Island will be your favorite place. Jeju Island is exotic enough to be called the Hawaii of Korea, where you can enjoy the beautiful nature to your heart's content. Jeju Island is famous for enjoying sea bathing and various outdoor activities on the beach.

Figure 14.1 Kyungbok Palace.

Credits

Fig. 14.1: Copyright © 2018 Pixabay/HeungSoon.

CHAPTER 15. COMPARING ITEMS AND TALKING ABOUT YOUR FAVORITES
제일 좋아하는 가수가 누구예요?

OBJECTIVES

- You will be able to compare two items and say which one you like better.
- You will be able to say your favorites in music, sports, food, and so forth.
- You will be able to ask and find out who knows the most about Korea.
- You will be able to talk about your favorite activity to do in your leisure time.
- You will be able to write about and present your favorite activity in your leisure time.

KEY EXPRESSIONS AND STRUCTURES

- N 보다 더: rather than N
- 제일/가장 Adj.: The most adj.
- 제일/가장 좋아하는 N: N that you like the most
- 취미가 뭐예요?: What's your hobby?

TASK: TALKING ABOUT YOUR FAVORITES

Ask about someone's favorites, such as their favorite singer, sport, food, restaurant, and leisure activity.

KEY PATTERN PRACTICE

Ask and answer the following questions about the city/state in which you currently live:

1. 인디애나에서 **제일 큰** 도시가 어디예요?
2. 인디애나에서 **제일 큰** 쇼핑몰이 어디예요?
3. 인디애나에서 학생들이 **제일 많은** 대학교가 어디예요?
4. 인디애나에서 **제일 재미있는** 놀이 공원이 어디예요?
5. 인디애나에서 물가가 **제일 비싼** 곳이 어디예요?

ACTIVITY 1: 뭐를 더 좋아해요?

Compare two items and choose which one you like better.

Figure 15.1 BTS

VS.

Figure 15.2 EXO

[보기]

김유진: 에밀리 씨, BTS 하고 Exo 중에서 누구를 **더** 좋아해요?

에밀리: 저는 BTS 를 **더** 좋아해요. 유진 씨는요?

김유진: 저는 **BTS 보다** Exo 를 **더** 좋아해요.

ITEMS	QUESTIONS	친구 1.	친구 2.	친구 2.
1. 코카콜라 vs. 펩시콜라	뭐가 **더** 맛있어요?			
2. 피자 vs. 햄버거	뭐를 **더** 좋아해요?			
3. 타겟 vs. 월마트	어디에 **더** 자주 가요?			
4. BTS vs. EXO	누구를 **더** 좋아해요?			
5. 수퍼맨 vs. 스파이더맨	누구를 **더** 좋아해요?			

ACTIVITY 2: 제일 좋아하는 것이 뭐예요?

Talk about your favorite singer, sport, restaurant, food, coffee shop, and class.

[보기]

김유진: 에밀리 씨가 **제일 좋아하는** 음식은 뭐예요?

에밀리: 저는 비빔밥을 **제일** 좋아해요. 유진 씨는요?

김유진: 제가 **제일 좋아하는** 음식은 떡볶이예요.

ITEMS	QUESTIONS	친구 1.	친구 2.	친구 3.
1. 가수	**제일 좋아하는** 가수가 누구예요?			
2. 운동	**제일 많이 하는** 운동이 뭐예요?			
3. 식당	떡볶이가 **제일 맛있는** 식당이 어디예요?			
4. 음식	**제일 좋아하는** 한국 음식이 뭐예요?			
5. 커피숍	**제일 자주 가는** 커피숍이 어디예요?			
6. 과목	**제일 좋아하는 과목**이 뭐예요?			

ACTIVITY 3: 한국에 대해서 제일 많이 아는 사람이 누구일까요?

Make a group of four and find out who knows the most about Korea. Decide by each member telling names of Korean movies, singers, dramas, and cities. When done, ask each group about who knows the most about Korea, as in the example.

> 한국 음식, 한국 영화, 한국 가수, 한국 드라마, 한국 도시

1. 한국 음식 이름을 **제일 많이 아는** 사람: _____

2. 한국 영화를 **제일 많이 본** 사람: _____

3. 한국 가수 이름을 **제일 많이 아는** 사람: _____

4. 한국 드라마를 **제일 많이 본** 사람: _____

5. 한국 도시 이름을 **제일 많이 아는** 사람: _____

[보기 1]

유진's Group: 에밀리 씨 그룹에서 한국 음식 이름을 **제일 많이 아는 사람**은 누구예요?

에밀리's Group: 데이빗 씨가 **제일 많이 알아요**.

[보기 2]

미나's Group: 마크 씨 그룹에서 한국 영화를 **제일 많이 본 사람**은 누구예요?

마크's Group: 수지 씨가 **제일 많이 봤어요.**

_____

_____

_____

_____

ACTIVITY 4: 제일 자주하는 활동은 뭐예요?

Talk about your favorite leisure activity.

[모델 대화]

김유진: 에밀리 씨는 **취미가 뭐예요?**

에밀리: 저는 **테니스 치는 걸** 제일 좋아해요. 유진 씨는요?

김유진: 저는 **요리하는 걸** 제일 좋아해요.

에밀리: 아, 그래요? 저도 **요리하는 것** 좋아해요.

김유진: 에밀리 씨는 무슨 요리를 제일 잘 해요?

에밀리: 저는 떡볶이를 제일 잘 만들 수 있어요. 유진 씨는요?

김유진: 저는 파스타를 제일 자주 만들어요.

_____

_____

_____

_____

_____

_____

_____

Wrap-Up Activity

Write about your favorite leisure activity. Include how often you do it, why you like doing it, how good you are at it, with whom you usually do it, and so forth. After writing, present your favorite activity to the class.

[모델 작문]

저는 시간 있을 때 자전거 타는 것을 제일 좋아해요. 일주일에 한 번쯤 자전거 타러 공원에 가요. 보통 룸메이트하고 같이 자전거를 타요. 저는 한 시간동안 탈 수 있어요. 자전거 타는 것은 재미있고 건강에 좋아요.

_____

_____

_____

_____

_____

_____

_____

_____

CULTURAL AWARENESS: KOREANS' HOBBIES 동호회 활동

Korean people have various hobbies, so there are many different groups called clubs for people with the same hobby to gather. People have regular meetings to enjoy their hobbies and to promote friendships with the people they met there. Nowadays, as the internet and smartphone apps become more common, it seems that more clubs are being formed because it is easy to make clubs and meet anywhere.

There are too many clubs with various hobbies to count, and there are many clubs that you can easily see everywhere, such as hiking clubs, morning soccer clubs, baseball clubs, ski clubs, singing clubs, travel clubs, and restaurant-visiting clubs. The clubs have regular meetings, but sometimes have instant meetings to meet more often because everyone uses a smartphone. There isn't any Korean who hasn't joined a club or two. What kind of club do you want to join if you go to Korea?

Figure 15.3 Biking.

Credits

Fig. 15.1: Source: https://www.flickr.com/photos/148669606@N03/33308711441/.
Fig. 15.2: Source: https://www.flickr.com/photos/138698601@N05/34127074750/.
Fig. 15.3: Copyright © 2015 Pixabay/Skeeze.

CHAPTER 16. PARTICIPATING IN A KOREAN SPEECH CONTEST
한국어 말하기 대회

OBJECTIVES

- You will be able to switch your speech style in a formal setting.
- You will be able to introduce yourself at a formal occasion.
- You will be able to write a script and rehearse for a Korean speech contest.

KEY EXPRESSIONS AND STRUCTURES

- V/A ~ㅂ/습니다: Formal ending used at a formal occasion and for a first-time encounter
- 처음 뵙겠습니다: It is the first time we've met!
- V~겠습니다: I'll V (Formal speech style)
- 시작하겠습니다: I'll begin
- 발표하겠습니다: I'll present

TASK: PARTICIPATING IN A KOREAN SPEECH CONTEST

Engage in formal-style speech for a formal occasion such as a student conference, a speech contest, talking to someone for the first time, and so on.

PRACTICE QUESTIONS

Ask and answer the following questions in deferential style ~ㅂ/습니다:

1. OO 씨는 어디에서 **왔습니까?**

2. 한국에 언제 **왔습니까?**

3. 지금 학교 기숙사에 **삽니까?**

4. 이번 학기에 무슨 수업을 **듣습니까?**

5. 왜 한국어를 **배웁니까?**

ACTIVITY 1: 한국 대학교에 교환학생으로 가서 자기소개 해 보세요.

Suppose that you are an exchange student at a university in Korea and you meet another exchange student in a Korean class. Ask about where the other student is from, when they came to Korea, where they are currently living, and so forth. Be sure to use formal language ~(ㅂ)/습니다 when meeting someone for the first time.

[모델 대화]

왕티엔:	안녕하**십니까?** 제 이름은 왕티엔**입니다. 처음 뵙겠습니다.**
에밀리:	네, 안녕하**십니까?** 저는 에밀리 잭슨**입니다. 반갑습니다!**
왕티엔:	에밀리 씨는 어디서 왔**습니까?**
에밀리:	저는 미국 인디애나에서 왔**습니다.** 티엔 씨는 어디서 왔**습니까?**
왕티엔:	저는 중국 상하이에서 왔**습니다.**
에밀리:	그럼 한국에 언제 왔**습니까?**
왕티엔:	2022 년 3 월에 왔**습니다.**
에밀리:	아, 그래요? 저는 지난 주에 왔**습니다.**
왕티엔:	그럼, 지금 학교 기숙사에 **삽니까?**
에밀리:	아니요. 저는 룸메이트하고 같이 아파트에 **삽니다.**

_____

_____

_____

_____

_____

_____

ACTIVITY 2: 학회 발표에서 자기 소개를 해 보세요.

Suppose that you go to a student conference. Introduce yourself before making a presentation and give a brief introduction about your presentation in front of the audience. Be sure to use formal language ~(ㅂ)습니다. You may use an English title when introducing your topic if technical terms are used.

[예시]

안녕하**십니까?** 제 이름은 김유진**입니다. 반갑습니다.** 저는 인디애나 대학교 2 학년**입니다.** 한국어하고 한국 문화를 전공하고 있**습니다.**

오늘 제 발표 주제는 '한국의 길거리 음식¹⁴'**입니다.** 그럼 발표를 시작하**겠습니다.**

_____

_____

_____

_____

_____

_____

_____

_____

¹⁴ '한국 길거리 음식': street foods in Korea

ACTIVITY 3: 학교 동아리에서 자기소개 해 보세요.

Suppose that you joined a university club this semester. Introduce yourself on the 1st meeting day. Include why you joined the club. Be sure to use formal language ~(ㅂ)/습니다 when meeting people for the first time.

[예시]

안녕하**십니까?** 제 이름은 에밀리 잭슨**입니다. 반갑습니다.** 저는 인디애나 대학교 2 학년이고 심리학을 전공하고 있**습니다.** 저는 한국 문화를 좋아해서 한국어를 잘 하고 싶**습니다.** '한국어 대화' 클럽에서 친구들도 사귀고 한국어를 많이 연습하고 싶**습니다.**

_____

_____

_____

_____

_____

_____

_____

ACTIVITY 4. 한국어 말하기 대회에 나가 보세요.

You are going to participate in the Korean speech contest. Write a script for your speech. You may choose any topic you want. After writing, rehearse the speech in front of the class.

The possible topics are the following:

- Why I study Korean
- My future dreams
- What my family means to me

<This is a script written by the winner of the beginner's level at the 2022 Korean speech contest>

제목: My future dream

안녕하십니까 여러분! 저는 언어학을 전공하는 대학교 1 학년 학생 한나 카틴스키 입니다. 오늘 저는 제 미래의 꿈에 대해 말씀 드리겠습니다. 일단, 저는 미래 꿈이 없습니다. 대신 미래 계획이 있습니다.

지금 저는 언어학을 공부합니다. 다른 많은 언어를 배우고 있는데 한국어를 제일 좋아합니다. 한국어하고 영어가 아주 달라서 한국어가 재미있습니다. 저는 지금 한국어 수업을 들으면서 한국 역사 수업하고 한국 문화 수업도 듣습니다. 이 수업들도 아주 재미있고 매일 새로운 것을 배웁니다.

미국 사람들이 한국어에 대해 많이 몰라서 저는 조금 슬픕니다. 나중에 저는 한국어의 역사를 연구하고 싶습니다. 그러면, 더 많은 미국 사람들이 한국어에 대해서 배울 수 있을 겁니다. 그런데 지금 저는 한국어를 잘 못 해서 할 일이 많습니다. 다음 학기도 계속 한국어 수업을 들을 겁니다. 그리고, 2023 년쯤 제가 3 학년 때 한국에 가고 싶습니다. 한국에 가서 한국어를 더 열심히 공부할 것입니다. 이것이 저의 미래 계획입니다.

제 발표를 들어 주셔서 감사합니다!

Script writer: Hannah Katinsky, Indiana University

제목:_____

CULTURAL AWARENESS: KOREAN ALPHABET DAY 한글날

October 9th is "Hangul Day" in Korea, which commemorates the day the new alphabet, Hangul, was created and published by King Sejong in 1446. On this day, various kinds of events and contests are held in order to widely spread the excellence and originality of Hangul. Korean essay and speech contests are the best available for students studying the Korean language. Topics of speech contests are usually given differently to each level. At the beginner level, they usually talk about their friends or family and their future dreams, and at the intermediate and advanced levels, they usually talk about Korean culture and experiences related to Korea.

Korean essay contests are usually held by submitting a book report after reading a selected book for the year. The selected books vary from school to school, but it is common to select books that have been translated and published in many other countries. When writing an essay, it is recommended to write it in Korean.

The winners of the contests usually get an award and a prize. Since you are learning Korean, why not participate in a contest and have a chance to show off your Korean skills as well as get a prize?

Figure 16.1 Korean speech contest.

www.ingramcontent.com/pod-product-compliance
Lightning Source LLC
Chambersburg PA
CBHW081436270326
41932CB00019B/3230